The
Quick-and-Easy
WEB SITE

BUILD A WEB
PRESENCE FOR YOUR
BUSINESS IN **ONE DAY**

PAULA PETERS

A
BUSINESS

Avon, Massachusetts

Published by Adams Business, an imprint of
Adams Media, an F+W Publications Company
57 Littlefield Street, Avon, MA 02322. U.S.A.
www.adamsmedia.com

ISBN 10: 1-59869-646-7
ISBN 13: 978-1-59869-646-2

Printed in Canada.

J I H G F E D C B A

Library of Congress Cataloging-in-Publication Data
is available from the publisher.

This publication is designed to provide accurate and authoritative information with
regard to the subject matter covered. It is sold with the understanding that the publisher
is not engaged in rendering legal, accounting, or other professional advice. If legal advice
or other expert assistance is required, the services of a competent professional person
should be sought.
—From a *Declaration of Principles* jointly adopted by a Committee of the
American Bar Association and a Committee of Publishers and Associations

Many of the designations used by manufacturers and sellers to distinguish their product
are claimed as trademarks. Where those designations appear in this book and Adams
Media was aware of a trademark claim, the designations have been printed with initial
capital letters.

This book is available at quantity discounts for bulk purchases.
For information, please call 1-800-289-0963.

➡ ACKNOWLEDGMENTS

I am very grateful to the many people who made this book possible—both in my business and personal lives. This book would not be possible without the help of some amazing people—friends, family, and colleagues alike.

To Ryan, I am so grateful for your support of this book—and of my writing career. I could not have completed this book without both your technical assistance, as well as your care of little Zachary, so that I could write and run my business. You have been a fabulous partner. And to Zachary—you will always be my "little boy."

To the technical experts who contributed to this book, I am very grateful: Mark Havran, my longtime friend and retired Webmaster; Mark Short, President of Transparent Solutions, Lisa Sizemore, my business colleague, client, and the president/founder of Hit Resultz; and Brody Dorland, my wonderful colleague, and owner of Something Creative, Inc.

To Lisa, I am so glad for all the joy and balance that you have given me with your friendship. Thank you for being such a supportive friend and fellow writer. To Michelle, our monthly lunches and your constant ideas for marketing my books have been a great help. I am indebted to my family for their constant words of encouragement, and for treating me like a "real writer": Audrée, Dick and Gerri, Joe and Christine, my nieces Tiajah, Viviana, and Mia, Jeff and Misty, Ann, Rich, Grandma Humrichouse, Aunt Dee, and Aunt Adrienne. Special thanks also go to my special supporters: Dale, Dugger, Aunie and Marty, Brenda and Scottie, Emily Hurtuk, Maria Suro, Alethea Cruz, Stacey and Sarah Allmandinger, Dr. Teri, all the girls from Debbie's Book Club—especially Cindy, Gail, Shelley I., Christy, Debbie, Michelle, Margaret—and the Lawrence Girls' Night

Group, including Lisa, Ellen, Xan, Melora, Barb, Theresa, Liz, Susan, and Marcia.

Many of my work colleagues through Peters Writing Services have been invaluable in the creation of this book, including Mary, Tammy, Lisa, Karla, and Mark—for their creative input, as well as support. And Sarah Holloway and Grandpa Rich have done a tremendous amount for our family, allowing me to accomplish this task.

To my consultant at the Small Business Development Center, Malinda Bryan-Smith, I can't thank you enough for your years of support for both my business and my book. Thank you for helping me locate the businesses who featured their samples in these pages.

Of course, I couldn't have gotten anywhere without my wonderful agent, Mike Snell, who several years ago convinced this nervous first-time author that, yes, I *could* finish a book—and I did. And then another one! And to my great editors at Adams Media: to Jill Alexander, it's been a joy to work with you once again; and to Laura Daly and Peter Archer, thank you for helping me get this manuscript off the ground. To Meredith O'Hayre and Brendan O'Neill, thank you for all of your hard work and edits, and for finally bringing this manuscript into the world as its very own book.

I am also grateful to the many clients and friends who gave me permission to use their samples in this book, which would not come alive without these samples. You have been a pleasure to work with. Thank you all so much for your help!

 # CONTENTS

→ INTRODUCTION

What if I told you that you could build a Web site for your business in only one day . . . for less than $500?

What if I told you that all you need is a computer, some basic computer experience, some software, and this book . . . along with a little elbow grease?

Maybe you'd call me crazy. "Don't you need an expensive Web design firm to create a nice Web site?" I can hear the skepticism in your voice. "Or at least, a decent *marketing* firm?"

You certainly *can* use a Web design firm or a marketing firm. There is nothing wrong with that. And for many people with time constraints and a larger budget, it is the perfect choice. But for your first Web site, you really don't *have* to. This book will show you how to do it yourself.

The Quick-and-Easy Web Site is designed to teach business owners how to create a standard, five-page Web site in as little as one day—for as little as $500. That's it. No fancy gadgets or tricks. No hard-core computer programming required. No knowledge of Flash or HTML necessary. Just simple, easy Web stuff.

What Do I Need to Create My Web Site?

- » A computer
- » Basic computer experience
- » Some software
- » This book
- » Elbow grease

In my business, Peters Writing Services, Inc., we help to create, design, and publish a lot of Web sites for our clients, thanks to the assistance of our wonderful graphic design and Web partners. Over and over again, I get asked by business owners, family, and friends, "What's the easiest way to get a Web site up and running?" The answers are right here, in this book.

If you have a small business that needs a Web site but do not have a large budget or a lot of time on your hands, this book is for you. It is also perfect for freelancers, organizations, associations, nonprofits, churches, and anyone else who needs a Web site up and running quickly and cheaply.

No matter what type of business you run, you will find the detailed instructions you need for creating—and marketing—your very own Web site. Whether you are a product business or a service business, a consulting business or a retail business, a longtime business or a brand-new startup, these chapters will walk you through the step-by-step process for creating your site, including planning it, creating it, marketing it, and then adding other functions to your site, such as blogs or shopping carts.

The actual creation of the Web site boils down to five simple steps. They are:

1. Purchase your domain name.
2. Write the Web content.
3. Design the page layout.
4. Find a Web host.
5. Publish the Web site.

In fact, even if you already have a Web site, but are ready to revamp it, you will still find plenty of good information here for adding functionality, redesigning, or rewriting your current pages. Maybe you want to add some new pages to it; or maybe you want to create a new graphic layout. Maybe you just need to market it a little better. Or maybe you are ready to add an online store (a big step!). Whatever your goals, you will find simple, easy-to-follow tips and techniques in this book.

You do not have to read this book front-to-back—you can use this book in any order that you'd like. If you just want to get down to the nitty gritty, and skip the discussion on planning, then go directly to Chapters 3 through 7, which cover the five easy steps to creating a basic Web page. If you prefer to spend more time planning, you'll find Chapter 2, "Plan a

Web Site for Your Business," to be worth a few minutes of your time. You may be interested more in the extra functions described in Chapter 4; or, you may be primarily interested in how to market your business with your Web site. This book does not need to be read in order, so pick the topic of your choice, and go for it.

How Quickly Can I Create My Web Site?

You can get a five-page Web site up and running in as little as one day, with less than $500. Simply follow the instructions in this book.

You may be wondering: how much computer experience is "basic" computer experience? How much computer experience do I *really* need to pull this off? Not as much as you might think. If you are familiar with standard, everyday software applications, such as word processing, e-mail, or Internet, you probably have enough experience to follow the instructions and create the five-page Web site recommended in this book.

The reality is that creating a Web site is not as hard as you might think. But most people are afraid to start because they are intimidated by the technology. However, with a few simple tools, just about anyone can do it—and it doesn't require a master's degree in Web design, or an understanding of computer programming, or a background in graphics. It doesn't even require a lot of money or time invested up front.

Let's get started!

Chapter 1

WHY DOES MY BUSINESS NEED A WEB SITE?

Y ou picked up this book, but maybe you are still unsure. You may be wondering, "Why does my business need a Web site? All we do is sell tumbleweeds. Who on earth cares about that?"

More people than you'd think. In fact, you may be surprised at just what a Web site can do for your business. Not only can it bring you more customers, but it can also increase your sales, open up new markets to you—and take your business to the next level.

But a Web site is a lot like a piece of new gym equipment. You buy it at the store, take it home, and then assemble it. But if you never use it, you'll never lose any weight or build any muscle.

A Web site is a powerful tool that can dramatically affect your business— but only if you use it properly. It starts with proper goal-setting, planning, mapping, and good execution. When you work with it, and really use it to its fullest potential, you will find unexpected results that you could only dream of.

The Story of a Skeptical Business Owner

I'd like to share a personal story with you. For years, even though I created Web content for many of my clients, I profoundly doubted the value of using a Web site in my own business. I'm embarrassed to admit it, but it's true.

For the past eight years, I have owned and actively managed a writing services business called Peters Writing Services, Inc. We have grown from one freelancer—me—into a small team of writers and designers that help small- and midsized businesses write government proposals, procedure manuals, training materials, and marketing materials. We help businesses who want to get high-quality writing without paying for a full-time writer or hiring an expensive marketing firm or ad agency.

When I first started out, my good friend and Webmaster extraordinaire Mark Havran suggested that I set up my own Web site. At the time, I was on a very tight budget, and was very skeptical about getting any return on my dollars invested, especially being a service-based business. I said, "Mark, this will never work. No one buys writing services over the Internet!"

But Mark persuaded me to give it a try, just to see what would happen. After all, I was spending a lot of time marketing myself at association meetings and trade shows; why not try this Web thing? So we set a budget of $500, and some reasonable goals about what we wanted to accomplish with this Web site. (At that time, Web pay-per-click marketing was still in its infancy, so I didn't even bother with that.) Our goal was to create a short Web site that would show my customers what we did, with a few samples. As I was new to the industry (and not yet creating Web sites for my own clients), I set a small budget, and in a month we published *www.peterswriting .com*. Shortly after I published it, I promptly forgot all about it.

About six months later, I noticed that new customers had stopped asking me for references (references are a big deal for new freelancers). As we signed the paperwork on a new project, I finally asked one of my clients, "Why didn't you ask me for a reference?"

He said, "I saw your Web site, I saw your samples, and I knew you were the real deal."

Suddenly, I realized . . . maybe we were onto something with this Web site. Sure enough, more and more people asked to see my Web site after I came in for a sales meeting. It was becoming a virtual sales portfolio. I could even refer to it on the phone when I couldn't get out to a location to visit with a customer.

My business is located in the southern suburbs of Kansas City. Out of the blue, about a year later, I got a call from a company in New Mexico. A secretary for a facilities management company was on the phone. "I'm looking for someone who can help us write a government proposal. Can you do it?"

"Yes, we write government proposals all the time for small companies like yours," I said, stunned. "How did you find us?"

 ## Never Doubt the Power of a Web Site!

No matter what kind of business you run—product, service, or even nonprofit—a Web site can do wonders for your sales. It can help you seal the deal, reach new customers, increase product sales, or find niche markets. It's a low-risk venture. And for only $500 and a day's worth of work—it's worth it to find out!

"We found your Web site on a Google search," she said. Suddenly, I realized this Web thing was even bigger than I had imagined. We ended up doing a major six-month project with the company, and we enjoy a good relationship with them to this day.

More calls came in, along the same lines. People had found us on the Internet and wanted to know more about our services. I knew that my Web site was paying off. But even though I'd had great success with the Web site bringing me new business and helping me to close deals, when my project manager (and husband) Ryan approached me about kicking off a full-blast pay-per-click ad campaign, I was again skeptical. "Sure, we need a Web site," I said. "But who on earth would really contact a writing service company in Kansas City, of all places, after doing a Google search?"

Happily, I was wrong again. After a slow first month, the calls and e-mails started coming in. One per week, two per week, and sometimes, five or six per week. I received inquiries about our services from Massachusetts, Texas, New York, and even Luxembourg!

Not all of these inquiries were good leads for us. In fact, about half were not a good fit. However, some of them turned out to be great project opportunities. And some of them were downright *perfect*.

Why am I telling you this embarrassing story about myself? I want to show you that no matter what kind of business you are in—whether it's products, services, or even nonprofit—a Web site can do wonders for your business. My goal is to get you to ask the question, "What can a Web site do for my business?"

You may just be surprised at the answer. And hey, for only $500 and a day's worth of work—isn't it worth it to find out?

What Can a Web Site Do for My Business?

Perhaps you are thinking—like I was—that a Web site is a waste of time. Perhaps you are a service-based business; or perhaps you aren't interested in selling products online. Maybe you think that your services are too complex to sell on a Web site.

Think again. Because you don't need to sell products to market your business online. In fact, my technical writing service business is an extremely complex service sale; I simply do not have an easy sales process. But my Web site has given me credibility, new leads, new customers, and great, profitable new projects. It has worked for many, many of my clients—in industries as diverse as electrical engineering to school transportation to financial estate management. And it can work for you, too. No matter whether you are a product business, a service business, a local business, or an international business—a Web site can benefit you in so many ways.

The Top Ten Things a Web Site Can Do for Your Business

What can a Web site do for your business? You will be amazed to find out. Here are my top ten favorite things that a Web site can do for any business:

#10—*Educate People About Your Business . . . Quickly*

Let's say you sell imported vases. You drop an e-mail to your Aunt Adrienne, out in Connecticut, knowing that she might be interested in your new turquoise products (or that her book club friends might be). You also know a few people from your last job who love antiques. What is the quickest, most low-pressure way to let them know about your new line of turquoise vases? Drop them an e-mail, say "hi," and include a link to your Web site.

A Web site is a quick, easy, nonintrusive way to educate people about your business. Friends, family, colleagues, current customers, and potential customers can easily learn all they need to know about your business—including new products or services—in sixty seconds or less, all while they are simply "window shopping"—which requires little or no commitment. After all, they are just reading their e-mail. What a powerful marketing tool!

#9—*Show That You Are a "Legitimate" Business*

One of the toughest challenges for any new business (especially a service business) is to show prospective customers that you are, indeed, a legitimate business—that you are here to stay. One way you can do that is by creating and operating a solid Web site.

Web sites act much like the storefronts and business cards of yesteryear: they signal to a new customer that you are a serious business owner, and that they can trust you. You are much less likely to be a fly-by-night operation if you are operating a Web site. This is especially critical for making those early sales that are so important to a new business.

#8—*Win New Prospects*

A big part of any marketing campaign is to find as many new prospects as possible. What is a prospect? It is a potential future customer who many not be ready to buy from you yet, but who is likely to need your products or services in the future. As you grow your business, you'll need as many new prospects as possible to convert into eventual customers.

Web sites are excellent tools for prequalifying prospects because they give a potential customer plenty of information to qualify themselves. This means that you spend less time with customers who are not serious about buying, or who don't have enough money to afford your products. Ideally, a well-written Web site should give a potential customer enough information about your product, price, service, and experience to realize that they need your help—before they ever speak to you or your staff.

#7—Put You on Par with Your Competitors

Whether or not you are seriously considering a Web site at this point, you can bet that your competitors are. Even if you don't believe that you are going to get much out of it as a marketing tool, it is worthwhile to have one up and running just to give you a fighting chance against your competitors.

Here's how it works: you just opened your upscale, jazzy restaurant, featuring steaks, seafood, and salads. You've worked for two years developing this concept, and you're proud of your location. There is only one other steak and seafood place in town—plenty of business for both of you.

A potential customer is trying to decide where to take her new boss for lunch. She wants something fancy, elegant, but not too expensive—the kind of place where she can impress her boss, without spending $100 on lunch. A jazzy restaurant with steaks and seafood would be perfect!

So while sitting at her desk that morning, she does a quick Internet search for steak and seafood restaurants in your area. She finds only one—your competitor! Even though their food quality is much poorer than yours, and the décor is much worse inside the restaurant, the owner took the time to create a brief, five-page Web site featuring pictures of their interior, their menu, a map to their location, and even a reservation system.

Ouch! There's one customer that you completely lost, just because your competitor had a Web site.

#6—Open Up a Whole New Market

The Internet has an amazing way of opening up entirely new—and often unconsidered—markets to you and your business. For my business, it opened up a national—and international—market that we hadn't previously considered. Up till that point, we mainly did business locally, in the Kansas City metro area. Putting up our Web site took us to another level; adding pay-per-click marketing took us to a higher level altogether.

Maybe you've been selling flower arrangements to hospitals in the Colorado Springs area for years. It's your specialty; you know the hospitals well, and you know just what flowers make the perfect fit for a family member or friend. But when you put your Web site up, you start getting calls from small office parks who want fresh flowers for their conference rooms, and hotels who like to put flower arrangements on the concierge's desk. *Voilà!* Suddenly you've got a whole new market that you hadn't even considered—and could not have found without your Web site.

#5—Give Credibility to Your Services

If you are primarily selling services, particularly expert-based services such as consulting, design, medical, legal, or financial services, credibility will always be a challenge. How do you show people that you have the experience to do the job?

The easy answer is: a Web site. A simple five-page Web site gives your customers an overview of your experience and services, using a client list, testimonials, and samples. People see in less than sixty seconds that you have the skills and experience to handle their toughest problems. And that's exactly what they want to know.

#4—Sell Products or Services

When it comes right down to it, a Web site is a great way to generate revenue. Best of all, it minimizes the face time required during the sale. It's also a great way to build trust in your sales to faraway customers, who may not be able to visit your store or office.

Even if you don't already have an office or storefront, you can start selling on the Web site today. It's that easy. But if you do already have a storefront, you can bring in additional revenue twenty-four hours a day, seven days a week.

#3—Tell Customers and Prospects About Your Products and Services

Maybe you have a product or service that is difficult to sell; perhaps it requires a lot of education for a customer about how it works, or perhaps it takes customers awhile to understand why it's better than the competing products on the market. If your product is complex or requires deep customer knowledge, a Web site is a perfect vehicle to communicate that—even if you are only selling your products off a shelf, or if you are still doing face-to-face sales meetings regarding your services.

Take health care products, for example. Over the last three years, many complicated, niche health care products have done very well with online sales. They simply take the time to educate potential customers about their products. They also sell their products through large commercial retail stores, such as Walgreen's and Target. For two great examples, check out Zanfel, a poison ivy wash (see *www.zanfel.com*), and Sinus Buster, a natural hot pepper nasal spray that relieves sinus pain and cluster migraines (see *www.sinusbuster.com*).

#2—Help Close the Deal

Even if you are selling complex services that would not easily translate to online sales, a Web site can still help you close the deal. Once you meet a potential customer for a sales meeting, your Web site can serve as a "credibility check" tool that helps you close the deal—either during the meeting, or after you leave, when the customer is learning more about you on their own.

 ## A Virtual Sales Folder

Many of my service business clients and colleagues use their Web site as a virtual sales folder. Instead of printing out a very expensive sales folder with a business card, a company profile, and samples, they now walk their customers through their Web site during the meeting—or leave a short, one-page flyer directing the customer to the Web site following their meeting. It pays for itself in saved printing expenses.

Since I put up my first Web site, I have had countless instances where my clients told me that my Web site helped them to make a final decision, often when I was bidding in a tight situation against several competitors. And our Web site isn't even that fancy! It was just enough to differentiate us from the other writing services out there, and show that we do good work.

That's the beauty of it: you don't have to have the *best* Web site on the Internet. You just have to have one that's available when your customer *needs* it.

#1—Win New Customers

Of course, the best thing a Web site can do for your business is to win you new customers—whether that's through direct sales, education, marketing, or word of mouth. A Web site can help you win new customers that you may never have found otherwise; it can also provide you with direct sales that you couldn't get through your storefront. That means more people spending money on your products and services. And that's exactly what every business needs.

What Is a Web Site . . . Really?

There's no shame in wondering, "What is a Web site . . . *really?*" Whether you're a new entrepreneur or an experienced businessperson, you may be new to the Web site game. And while you may have nailed down the other marketing materials that are important to a business—such as logos, business cards, stationery, and brochures—you may still be wondering about the nuts and bolts of that electronic giant, *the Internet.*

In that case, I'm here to reassure you: a Web site is nothing mysterious at all. In fact, it's something you can easily learn to create yourself.

Here's what a Web site is *not:* It's *not* a complicated computer program. It's *not* high-falutin' database wizardry. In fact, a Web site is nothing more than a brochure or catalog, in an electronic format.

Sound simple? It is. In fact, it is very similar to many other marketing materials that you may already be using—just in a different format. Instead of colored paper, or a business card, or a billboard, you are creating an electronic brochure that communicates the information about your business to your new customers on a computer screen.

A Web site is a simple, electronic medium that gives customers the opportunity to learn about your business from the privacy of their home or office—without visiting your store or company. But it's more than that—it's also an amazing way for people all across the globe to buy your products and services. No matter where you operate your business—whether it's in Missoula, Montana, or Seboomook, Maine—you can advertise yourself to potential customers who need to buy your products and services. Now, isn't that incredible?

Ye Olde "Wild West" Web Days

Back even a few years ago, you had to be an expert computer programmer to get a Web site up and running— and creating one was difficult, expensive, time-consuming, and, yes—downright scary. But all that has changed. It's no longer the Wild West Web. Today, there are many inexpensive, readily available tools on the market that allow you to create your own Web site. Many of these easy tools are suggested throughout this book—take advantage of them whenever you can, to save you time and money.

The Amazing Growth of the Internet . . . and How It Helps You

The good news is that since the Internet has grown so quickly over the past few years, there is a very high demand for new, easy-to-use tools to create Web sites. What does that mean for you? That means that today, right now, it's easier (and cheaper) than ever to create your own Web site.

According to a March 2007 Netcraft survey, there are more than 110 million Web sites up and running across the world. Believe it or not, as early as April of 1997, there were only 1 million Web sites up and running; but by May 2004, that number jumped to 50 million. That's 49 million new Web sites in only seven years!

The reason that the Internet has exploded is because *Web sites have gotten easier to create.* In the "old days," you needed to be an expert computer programmer to get a Web site up and running. You needed to know complicated programming language to even get started. Today, however, all you need is some easily available software, the simple instructions included in this book, one day, and $500 . . . and *voilà*! You are ready to publish your own Web site.

Web Site vs. Brochure/Catalog

Still hesitant about creating your own Web site? Here's another reason to try it: it actually costs less than designing and printing 1,000 copies of an 8.5" x 11" trifold brochure, and less than 500 copies of a standard twenty-page product catalog.

Still not convinced? A Web site lasts longer than a brochure or catalog, saves on paper waste, and reaches more people. And it never needs to get outdated—it can instantly be updated with new products, customer testimonials, or contact information—without any additional reprinting expense. Try *that* with a traditional brochure or catalog!

So What's the Bottom Line?

The bottom line is this: a Web site is an electronic brochure or catalog for your business. Believe it or not, it's actually *less expensive* to create a Web site than to design and print a catalog or brochure—and it will last longer, too. And unlike a paper brochure or catalog, a Web site can instantly be updated to add new products, customer testimonials, or contact information. It is more interactive and entertaining than a traditional brochure. And best of all—it can reach more people, in more far-flung places, than ever before. In fact, you can reach customers you didn't even know existed!

So strap on your seat belt, and get ready for your first big step: planning the right Web site for your business.

Chapter 2

PLAN A WEB SITE FOR YOUR BUSINESS

No matter how much of a rush you are in to build your Web site, it is worthwhile to take thirty minutes to develop a plan for it. That thirty-minute investment may prevent two hours of frustration later, if you get "stuck" in the midst of your design.

🕐 Total Time: 30 minutes

For example, even if you need to finish your Web site *today*, a good Web site map will do wonders for you (see section in this chapter called "Create a 'Site Map.'" It will save you wasted time writing pages you don't need or adding useless navigation links that you will only have to remove later. The exercises in this chapter should only take you a few minutes to complete, but you will cherish those few minutes later, when you are relaxed and ready to publish your site "live."

💲 Total Cost: $0

However, if you are *really* short on time and are willing to stick to the basics, skip the custom planning section—and go directly to "The Basic, Five-Page Web Site" section, at the end of this chapter. That will give you an entire outline for creating an industry-standard, five-page, basic Web site that will get you up and running.

Understand Your User

Why is it so important to understand your user? Because every business has a unique customer that buys from them. And just like tailoring a storefront for your best customers, you'll want to customize your Web site for your best users—including the content, graphics, and navigation.

The more comfortable your user feels browsing your Web site, the more likely they are to visit it repeatedly. It increases the likelihood of sales, as well as referrals to friends, which results in more sales. And that's the name of the game—*sales*.

B2B vs. B2C

Do you sell to businesses . . . or consumers?

If you sell to businesses, you are called a B2B (shorthand for "business-to-business") company. If you sell directly to individual persons, you are called a B2C company (or "business-to-consumer").

If your customers do not get a good feeling from your Web site, they won't buy from you. And if they don't buy from you, your Web site is a waste of time. It makes no difference whether you are selling products, services, or association memberships. A Web site *must* "connect" with your target audience to be effective.

For example, a Web site selling medical supplies (such as infant Motrin) to pediatric clinics may have a very different user than a Web site selling the exact same medical supplies to first-time moms. See the difference? A director of operations at a clinic with 500 pediatric patients each day will be looking for very different things than a first-time mom with a newborn. As you can imagine, each one of those Web sites will require a different writing style, amount of content, and graphic design.

Your customers are your users. The good news is, you probably already know quite a bit about your customers. Now, all you need to do is capture that information, and summarize it.

Who Are Your Customers?

Have you ever thought about your customers before? I mean . . . really, *really* thought about your customers? If not, now is the perfect opportunity. Think about the people who buy your products or use your services. Who are they? What do they do in their spare time? Where do they work? What are their personalities usually like? By keeping these preferences in mind, you can tailor your graphics and content as much as possible to that target audience.

If you sell directly to individuals, you are a B2C company. If you sell directly to businesses, you are a B2B company. Even if you sold the exact same product—such as custom engraved pens—you would want to use different graphics, content, and even layout for each audience. After all, a business customer is looking for something that relates to her business, while a consumer is looking for something for herself, family, or friends.

 ## What If I Don't Have Any Customers Yet?

Don't sweat it if you don't have any customers yet. First, imagine exactly who you want to buy from you. Be as vivid as you can in your imagination. What kind of customers will be buying your products and services? Who would you most like to work with? What do they look like? Where do they work? What kinds of hobbies do they have? Create a picture in your head of the ideal customer. Then follow the same instructions for this exercise.

Think about your best customers. Who do you enjoy doing business with? Who would you like to do *more* business with? Picture your ideal, favorite customers, the ones you wish you had 1,000 more of. Now, think about:

- » Are they businesses or individual consumers?
- » Where do they work?
- » Where do they live?
- » What are their needs?
- » Do they have family?
- » What are their favorite activities?
- » What stage are they at in their lives?
- » What goals are they trying to accomplish?
- » What products or services do they typically buy from you?

Of course, not all your customers will fall into the same category. You will find a lot of variation, even among your regular customers. But I find that most businesses—even the smallest ones—notice a "profile" among their repeat customers. They tend to have the same jobs, wear the same kinds of clothes, work in the same industry, provide the same services, or be at the same stage in their lives. Why? Because most likely, your products and services appeal to a certain group of people, or a certain segment of businesses.

Now that you have a certain group of customers in mind, think about what they are like. How would you describe them? Jot down your ideas in the space provided, and be as detailed as possible.

For B2C businesses, include age, income level, marital status, career choice, number of children, hobbies, home location—anything you might possibly know about their habits and buying patterns. For B2B businesses, include the number of employees, size of revenue, industry type, business location, department that usually buys from you—anything that will help you identify who the business is.

Describe Your Customers in Detail
My typical customer:

_____

_____

_____

_____

Describe Your Customers' Preferences
Now, take sixty seconds to describe your customers' preferences. Think about who you are doing business with. What will they want in a Web site?

Check the keyword for each category below that best describes your client. If you don't see the right word, write in one of your own.

Your Typical Customers' Preferences
My customer is a . . .

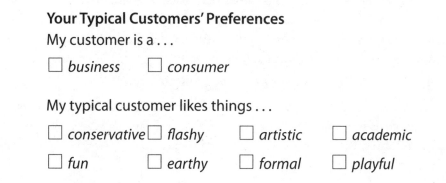

☐ business ☐ consumer

My typical customer likes things . . .

☐ conservative ☐ flashy ☐ artistic ☐ academic

☐ fun ☐ earthy ☐ formal ☐ playful

☐ scientific   ☐ simple   ☐ homey

☐ _____ (other)

My typical customer's Web experience level is . . .

☐ savvy   ☐ average   ☐ okay   ☐ nonexistent

☐ _____ (other)

My typical customer prefers to read . . .

☐ tons of text ☐ lots of text ☐ some text ☐ very little text

☐ hardly any text   ☐ _____ (other)

My typical customer enjoys . . .

☐ tons of graphics   ☐ lots of graphics

☐ some graphics   ☐ very little graphics

☐ hardly any graphics   ☐ _____ (other)

You now have a basic guide to help you make design and content decisions going forward. If your typical customer is earthy, with very little Web experience, you'll want to create a Web site that is very simple to use, and uses earthy tones for colors—such as browns and greens. If your average customer is scientific and enjoys reading lots of text, consider using some scientific imagery, specific shapes (such as squares and rectangles), and more detailed page content.

As you move through this book, refer back to these preferences again and again to help you make decisions—such as whether to use bullets or long paragraphs; photos or simple graphics; and fun and flashy fonts, or more conservative, businesslike fonts.

Set Reasonable Goals for Your Web Site

As part of your planning process, you will benefit from taking a few minutes to set goals for yourself. Don't just mindlessly throw your Web site up on the Internet. What are you trying to achieve?

Buy Your Domain Name Now

Even though you are only in the planning stages for your Web site—and it may be awhile before you finish it—you would be wise to purchase your domain name now. It is fairly inexpensive to do, and the best names go quickly. If you decide not to create your Web site, you can always let the name go later, at no penalty to you.

Even if you are only considering creating a Web site at some point, I strongly recommend that you take this step. Purchase your domain name for a year. You can always renew it later. For more instructions on the domain name purchase, check out Chapter 3, "Step 1: Purchase Your Domain Name."

Lofty goals may actually hurt your motivation. Be reasonable. If you can communicate the message about your business in five pages, stick with five pages. You don't need ten just to make a bigger splash. In fact, one of our guidelines in creating Web sites at Peters Writing Services is: the shorter, the better. If you can only handle one sale per day, don't set a goal of five per day. The idea is to set goals for your Web site that you can comfortably meet. You can always shoot higher—*later*. Not only that, but the smaller the site, the faster it will be up and running.

When I set out to create a Web site for a new client, I spend a good amount of time in the initial interview learning about their goals. Do they want to sell more products? Do they want to show off how much experience they have? Or, do they simply want to get a quick Web site "out there" to be on par with a competitor? All these are valid, reasonable goals for a business.

Here are a few of the questions I ask a new client about the goals for their Web site:

> » How will you use this Web site in your sales process?
> » What do you want this Web site to do for your business?
> » Are you interested in using the Web site to market your business?

> » Will you measure the results that you get from using your Web site?
> » Do you want your site to be fancy, or simple?
> » What are your competitors doing with their Web sites?

What Is a Sales Cycle?

A "sales cycle" is how you sell your products or services. Most retail businesses have the same sales cycle: a customer enters the store, finds their product, and brings it to the register. Total sales cycle: thirty minutes.

In the case of a consulting business, however, it may be more complicated: they perform an analysis of the customer's needs, hold a sales meeting with the customer, present an estimate, then sign a working agreement. The service is performed, and the customer pays. Total sales cycle: six months.

Ask yourself the same questions. What are you hoping your Web site will do for you? The answers to these questions will help guide you through the process of creating your own Web site.

Once you have defined your goals, you may even be thinking that you want to measure your performance on your goals. This helps you to find out your return on investment (called "ROI" in the marketing business) for your investment of time and money in the Web site.

For example, if you spend $500 creating your Web site, and another $250 marketing it through different media (such as pay-per-click advertising and a weekly ad in your hometown newspaper), you've spent $750 on your Web site. If you sell $2,000 worth of purple teddy bears in the first year as a result of your Web site, you have come out ahead—you could comfortably say you have had a good return on investment of $1,250. However, if you only sell $100 worth of purple teddy bears, than you may decide that the Web site was not a worthwhile investment. Or—perhaps it tells you that you should structure your Web site differently, or use it differently in your advertising.

However, don't feel pressured at this point to measure your performance against your goals. My biggest fear when I teach new entrepreneurs in my marketing classes is that that they will get so hung up on measurements, that they will get too scared to take the next step. So much of business success lies in taking decisive action.

So don't get bogged down with the details. Measuring your goals is less important than getting your Web site up and running. You can save measurement and reporting for when you are more established with your business.

Of course, the other point is that the return you get from your Web site can't always be measured in dollars. Although I can't point to a dollar figure, I am certain that getting my Web site up and running within the first few years of starting my business won me several projects I could not have won without it.

How do I know this? Because of feedback from my clients. Several of my clients told me later that they were impressed with my Web site, and that it gave me credibility—so I know that it influenced their decision. You may eventually feel the same way about your Web site, too.

Examples of Reasonable Web Site Goals

What are reasonable goals to set for a new Web site? Here are a few of the most common goals for a small business or organization, looking to establish a new Web presence (of course, yours may differ from these, and that's fine, too):

1. Sell products online
2. Increase credibility
3. Get new leads
4. Educate customers
5. Compete with other businesses
6. Improve visibility of the business
7. Just get the darn thing up and running (yes, that is a valid reason—because you just know it's the right thing to do for your business; listen to your gut!)

Now, try setting some goals for your own business or organization. In the exercises below, choose one or two goals that seem right for you, and fill in the blanks. This two-minute exercise will clarify your motivation for creating your site, and save you frustration later on, when you are trying to determine whether or not it is working for you.

Keep in mind that you don't have to do all these goals—or even many of them. Just choose the one that fits best for you, and fill in the blanks for yourself.

Goal #1: Sell My Products Online

Maybe you have a storefront; maybe you don't. Either way, you are ready to start selling your products online. How many products would you like to sell in a week? A month? A year? There is no right or wrong answer here. For some businesses, such as custom art businesses, selling one product a year is ideal; for others, it will be thirty per day. Whatever is right for you, jot it down. Be as specific as you can.

> **Example:**
> I would like to sell four antique dolls every day.
>
> I would like to sell one major project every month.
>
> I would like to sell _____ every _____.

Goal #2: Increase My Credibility

If you are a service professional, and your business depends on people having confidence in your experience, your main goal in creating a Web site may be to increase your credibility with prospective customers. This is especially true for specialists, such as artists, lawyers, writers, mediators, and medical professionals.

In this case, your goal might be:

> I would like to show my customers that I am an excellent artist who works in several different media.
>
> I would like to show my customers that I am the best racing motorcycle mechanic in the entire Honolulu area.
>
> I would like to show my customers that I am:
>
> _____

Goal #3: Get New Prospective Customers

If you are using your Web site to generate new prospective customers for you, you may wish to set a goal for the number you find. A "prospective customer" is simply one who is interested in you; they may or may not end up buying from you. This goal could be specific, using numbers; or it could be more general, just to get you moving in the right direction.

For example:

> I would like my Web site to generate three new prospective customers for my business each week.
>
> I would like my Web site to generate some calls to my store from interested customers.
>
> I would like my Web site to generate:
>
> _____

Goal #4: Educate My Customers

Perhaps your goal is simply to educate customers—either about your business, about trends in the world, or about new products. Either way, you have a message they need to hear.

Ask yourself, "What is the message that I want to communicate? What do they need to know?"

> I would like my Web site to educate my customers about the new tax laws about vehicle purchase that can seriously affect their income.
>
> I would like my Web site to educate my customers about how my spaghetti pot will save them from overcooked pasta.
>
> I would like my Web site to educate my customers about:
>
> _____

Goal #5: Compete with Other Businesses

You may just need to get a Web site up and running because your competitors have one. That's a perfectly good reason to have one—you may be losing market share because you are invisible to customers who are searching for you online, or who can find your competitors more quickly using the Internet. This is especially applicable in the hospitality industry, where restaurants and B&Bs without Web sites are quickly losing customers to their competitors who offer menu previews and online photos of their facilities.

In this case, your goal will be straightforward:

> I would like to establish my Web site so that I can compete effectively with the Happy Inn & Suites that just opened up in town.

> I would like to establish my Web site so that I can compete effectively with all the established restaurants in the Printer Row district.

> I would like to establish my Web site so that I can compete effectively with

> _____

Goal #6: Improve the Visibility of My Business

Perhaps you want to use your Web site in coordination with an entire marketing campaign. Or, perhaps you are just trying to improve the general visibility of your business in your town, state, or region. That is also a perfectly acceptable goal.

> I would like to use my Web site so that small banks and credit unions in the financial industry in the Dallas/Ft. Worth metro area get to know my business.

> I would like to use my Web site so that volleyball fanatics in the Eastbrooke neighborhood area get to know my business.

> I would like to use my Web site so that_____ in the

> _____ area get to know my business.

Goal #7: Just Want to Get the Darn Thing Up and Running

As an entrepreneur, you live by your "gut feelings." And maybe your gut is telling you: you'd better get a Web site up and running—soon. That's perfectly legitimate. It's okay to say: we need to get a Web site going to make our business feel like—well, a real business!

If your main goal is just to get a Web site up and running as quickly as possible, set a reasonable goal, such as to be published by a certain date. If you are unsure of how many pages to include, just go for the basic five pages. For example:

> I would like to get my five-page Web site up and running by December 5th.
>
> I would like to get my eleven-page Web site up and running by Monday morning.
>
> I would like to get my _____-page Web site up and running by_____.

Now What?

Now that you have your goals written out, what do you do with them? You use them to help guide your decisions as you write, design, and publish your site. Keep them handy as you work through this book. I like to hang them up on a bulletin board above my desk, or keep them in the project folder for the client I am working with.

You may also find that your goals can help you reevaluate your Web site after it's been up and running for a few months. So, tuck them away somewhere. Put them in your planner, or your calendar, or a folder you'll look at later on. After three months, or six months, or twelve months, revisit your goals. Ask yourself, "Am I meeting my goals? Did I accomplish what I set out to? How are my goals different now?" You may even want to schedule some future time on your calendar to review these questions.

When you get to that future date, you may say, "Wow! Look how much I accomplished in such a short period of time." Or you may say, "Boy, I'd really like to get even *more* out of this Web site. How do I do *that?*" Either way, a future review helps you make sure that your goals are still working for you—and gives you the opportunity to write new ones.

Create a "Site Map"

Whether you want a grand production, or a simple setup, you will benefit from taking the time to draw out a visual map of your Web site (called a "site map"). With a visual representation of what your final Web site will be, it will be easier to write, design, and publish your final version.

What Is a Site Map?

A site map is a visual picture of all the pages on your Web site. This allows you to plan the total number of pages in your final Web site, including the titles, topics, navigation, and any subpages. The best professionals use these, but you can do it, too, just by drawing it freehand on a piece of paper. Once you've finished, you've got a "map" for moving forward on the content and design.

Paper vs. Computer

It doesn't matter whether you create your site map on the computer or by hand. The important thing is just getting your ideas down.

If you use a computer to do your site map, any software program that creates simple drawings (such as PowerPoint or Microsoft Word) should work fine. My favorite program for creating site maps (and the one I used to create the examples you see here) is Visio, a software tool for technical writers that allows you to create organizational charts and schematic maps. But Visio is expensive, and can be difficult to learn; you don't really need it. Choose whatever tool works best for you.

Proposed Layout for Peters Writing Services Web Site

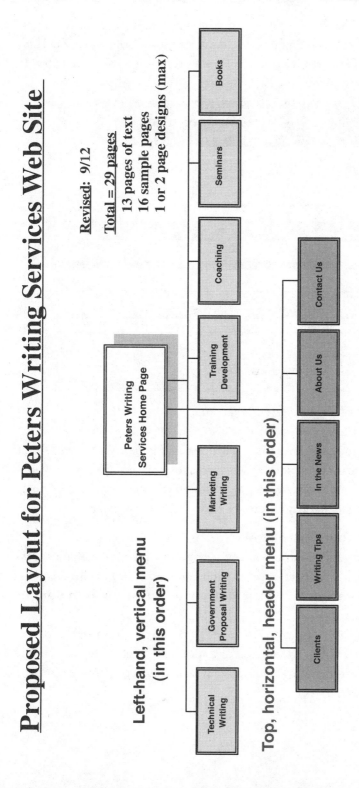

Revised: 9/12

Total = 29 pages
13 pages of text
16 sample pages
1 or 2 page designs (max)

Left-hand, vertical menu (in this order)

- Technical Writing
- Government Proposal Writing
- Marketing Writing

Peters Writing Services Home Page

- Training Development
- Coaching
- Seminars
- Books

Top, horizontal, header menu (in this order)

- Clients
- Writing Tips
- In the News
- About Us
- Contact Us

Site map for revision of *www.peterswriting.com*
Courtesy of Paula Peters and Peters Writing Services, Inc.

Now that we have been writing and designing Web sites for our clients for several years, our site map process has gotten more sophisticated. This past year, when I was ready to revamp *www.peterswriting.com* yet again, I used our newer template. Our new site map looked like this:

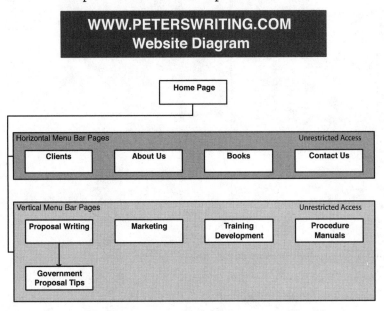

Later revision of *www.peterswriting.com*

Courtesy of Paula Peters, Ryan Humrichouse, and Peters Writing Services, Inc.

You can do the exact same thing with pen and paper. We only use the software template for presentation purposes. You can simply draw up your own boxes and squares with your page titles on it. In fact, we usually do a hand-drawn version anyway before we create it in our software.

Now Create Your Own Site Map

Now that you've seen mine, it's your turn to try. Take out a blank sheet of white paper, a blank sheet of lined paper, and a pen or pencil. This will give you an opportunity to get your ideas out on the page in both a linear and a visual fashion.

On the lined sheet of paper, jot down all the topics you need to cover on your Web site. Think about this for a moment. What information do you want your customers to see about your business? Try to come up with at least five topics.

Let's imagine for a moment that you own a business repairing motorcycles. Your business name is Jeff's Custom Cycles. Your list might include:

Stuff to Include in My Web Site

» Repair services
» Location and hours of operation
» Info about the shop
» Mechanics who work here
» Why we're awesome

That's a great start to a Web site. Do the same thing on your sheet of lined paper.

When you are done with your list, take one more minute and write the corresponding Web page title next to your list. For each topic, you should come up with one common Web page name. This should not be hard—think of all the common Web pages you know, including the home page, contact us page, and services or products page. Assign each item on your list to a common Web page category.

The Five-Page Web Site

If you are planning to just create a standard, five-page Web site, you are welcome to use these page titles:

» Home page
» Services/products page
» Clients page
» About us page
» Contact us page

These are described in more detail in the next section, "The Basic, Five-Page Web Site."

For example, the list for Jeff's Custom Cycles now becomes:

Stuff to Include in My Web Site

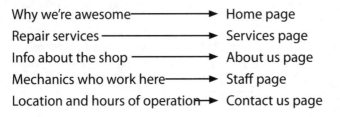

Repair services ⟶ Services page
Location and hours of operation ⟶ Contact us page
Info about the shop ⟶ About us page
Mechanics who work here ⟶ Staff page
Why we're awesome ⟶ Home page

See? That's not so hard. If we rearrange them in order, by most important to least important, the list now becomes:

Order of Web Pages

Why we're awesome ⟶ Home page
Repair services ⟶ Services page
Info about the shop ⟶ About us page
Mechanics who work here ⟶ Staff page
Location and hours of operation ⟶ Contact us page

Common Web Page Names

Some of the most common Web page names include:

- » Home page
- » Services page
- » Products page
- » About us page
- » History page
- » Careers page
- » Clients page
- » In the news page
- » Success stories page
- » Contact us page

Be creative. You are not limited to these page titles. Feel free to come up with your own unique pages!

Notice that the home page always comes first, and the contact us page comes last.

Now, it's your turn. Put your pen to the paper, and quickly assign each topic that you listed to a Web page category. If you are stuck for the moment, don't sweat it. Just leave it blank, and come back to it later.

When you are done assigning each topic to a Web page category, rearrange them in order. Remember to put the home page first, and the contact us page last.

When you are finished with your list, you are ready to draw your site map. Pull out your blank piece of white paper. You will draw one box for each page title that you listed on your sheet of lined paper.

To keep it organized, stick to these rules:

» 1 topic = 1 page = 1 box
» Home page at the very top

Don't try to squeeze too much into each box. If you have subtopics that need to be addressed, draw separate boxes. These will become subpages later. For now, all you need to know is that one box can align to one topic.

Put your home page at the very top. Now draw connector lines out to all the rest of the boxes. All your other boxes can lead out from the home page, in a single row.

For example, the drawing for Jeff's Custom Cycles now looks like:

Jeff's Custom Cycles

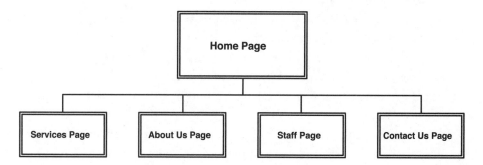

Sample Web site map for Jeff's Custom Cycles

Don't make it more complicated than it is. We're just talking about drawing lines and squares!

Site Map for the Basic Five-Page Web Site

If you are planning to do the basic, five-page Web site suggested in this book, your site map will be pretty simple. In fact, you are welcome to use mine:

The Basic, 5-Page Web Site

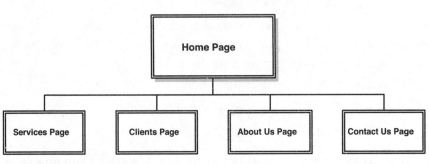

Basic, five-page Web site map

Courtesy of Paula Peters and Peters Writing Services, Inc.

Now it's your turn. Draw out your site map on the blank piece of paper. Remember to put one topic in each box, and don't overcrowd it. After all, you only need one page to make a Web site—so it doesn't have to be big, fancy, or impressive! The goal is to create a simple drawing that will help guide you later, when you are ready to write and lay out your Web site.

Revise Your Site Map

When you are finished drawing out your Web site map, walk away from it for a little while. (Yes, that's right . . . walk away from it!)

Why? Because you may have an overly ambitious site map. Or, you may not have as much on paper as you've had in your head. Either way, it helps to leave it alone, even if only for five minutes, and come back to it for a quick revision.

So put the papers aside, go for a cup of coffee, have lunch, or, if you have time, sleep on it and come back tomorrow. You may even want to show it to a spouse, partner, friend, or colleague for feedback.

When you see it again, how do you feel about it? Does it look too "busy"? Are there too many boxes there? Or does it look too empty, like there is not as much as you wanted?

If your best friend looks at it for a few minutes, nods, and then says, "Wow, you've sure got a lot on here," then maybe you are tackling too much on your first draft. Remember—it's much easier to start out with a smaller Web site, and add more later, than to start with twenty or thirty pages and get too overwhelmed.

Start Small

It is always better to start out with a smaller Web site and grow it. The more pages you add, the more work it will take. Besides, it's easy to add pages later, even after you've published your site.

When someone comes to me wanting a behemoth, 100-page Web site, part of my job is to help them clarify their goals and reduce their page count. This reduces wasted time, money, and effort, and often saves their sanity during a long Web overhaul project.

Take another stab at it. Delete a few boxes, if you need to. Reduce some of the clutter. Add any boxes that you feel are missing. Remember, every one of those boxes means time spent writing and designing and publishing— and you are a busy entrepreneur. If you don't really need it, scratch it. You can always add more pages later, *after* you've published your Web site.

When you are done revising your site map, you have a nice, simple plan for writing, designing, and publishing your Web site. You will use this again and again throughout the book, and for the life of your business. Congratulations!

What If I Am Really Stumped on My Site Plan?

If you are really stumped with designing a site plan for your Web site, have no fear. You can always use my site plan for a basic, five-page Web site, included in the next section of this chapter. It makes site planning a no-brainer.

Read on to learn more about the basic, five-page Web site.

The Basic, Five-Page Web Site

Over the years of Internet growth, I have observed a trend: the five-page Web site. It is easy, simple, fast, and possible to create in one day. And it has also become an industry standard, especially for new or growing businesses. If you are stumped, confused, or in a rush, start with these basic five pages—and you can't go wrong.

 What If I Want More than Five Basic Pages?

Relax—you can always use these five pages to get you started, then build on it later. The five-page Web site is a great starter that covers all the bases. Later, you can add as many pages as you'd like.

In my experience, the five basic pages include:

> » Home page
> » Services/products page
> » Clients page
> » About us page
> » Contact us page

These five pages should give your customers enough information about your business to decide whether or not to buy from you. Remember, a Web site is a brochure for your business, just like anything else—and just like a paper trifold brochure that you might hand out at a trade show. You want to educate your customers, without overloading them with too much information.

Here is a brief overview of the content your five-page Web site should include on each page.

Home Page

A home page is a quick summary that tells your customer why they should do business with you. It usually includes a list of benefits, a short description of your company, and some basic information about the services you provide.

In short, a home page should tell your customer—in two paragraphs or less—that you are the right person for the job. This is the place to sell yourself. It is also the "jumping-off point" for the entire Web site, and shows the customer a little bit about your business personality through the graphic design.

Services/Products Page

The services/products page describes what you do. What services do you provide to your customers? Or, what products do you sell? Some companies do both, and that's okay, too.

This page shows off exactly what wares you sell in your business, usually in the form of a list, photos, or descriptions. It's a great opportunity to differentiate yourself from your competition.

Clients Page

The clients page tells us who your customers are. It's very simple. Most businesses do this in the form of the list. Some also use paragraphs to describe who their customers are, and how their products or services assist them. You can handle it any way you choose.

The bottom line is, prospective customers want to know who else does business with you. The bigger the list of names, the better. (We'll talk about getting the company's permission in Chapter 4.)

About Us Page

Every company has a story to tell about their business. The about us page tells your customers about your company, its history, and its people. It can be elaborate—with lots of detail about why you founded the company, bios of the people who work for you, and your mission statement—or it can be simple, with just a couple of sentences about why you do the work that you do, and what makes you passionate about it.

Contact Us Page

This is the simplest page of the five. As you might have guessed, the contact us page has exactly that—the contact information for your company. This typically includes your phone number, business address, personnel information, and—if necessary—directions or a map to your facility.

Site Map for a Basic Five-Page Web Site

The site map for a basic five-page Web site is just as simple as the content is. You can see it on page 32. You now have a content overview and a site map for your basic five-page Web site. That's plenty to get you started. (Now, that's what I call an *instant* Web site!)

You are now ready to move on to step one in creating your Web site: purchasing your domain name, if you haven't already done so (see Chapter 3, "Step 1: Purchase Your Domain Name").

What If These Pages Are Not Right for My Business?

Just because I suggest these five standard Web site pages, it doesn't mean you *have* to use them. Don't let my suggested site map limit your creativity.

When a client comes to me, and says, "Paula, I need a Web site, but I don't know what on earth to put in it," then we usually start with the five basic pages. We may end up staying with just the original five pages, or we may add tons of other pages. In fact, many times, my clients and colleagues publish their initial Web site with just these five pages, then grow it to become ten or fifteen pages later on. It can happen organically like that for you, too, and that's fine. That's a normal part of the process.

If these five particular pages don't work for you or for your clients, choose ones that are more appropriate for your business. Take the time to create a site map of what you are looking for (see the previous section in this chapter, "Create a 'Site Map'"). Or, check out the common other pages listed in Chapter 4, under "Common Additional Pages."

For example, a success stories page may show off your services better than a clients page. Or, maybe you don't have any clients yet—perhaps you are just starting out—and a how-it-works page would suit you better. Maybe you are a freelance artist or writer who would do better to show off a portfolio of your work. If that's the case, do it. In each of those cases, you can use the "Common Additional Pages" section in Chapter 4 for ideas.

Beware of Plagiarism!

While you are planning your Web site, you may spend time surfing the Internet to check out other business Web sites. It's fine to get ideas from other sites for your content and design—but you never want to plagiarize. "Plagiarizing" means stealing other people's content, designs, images, photos, or ideas. The last thing you want to do is spend your first year in business fending off copyright litigation about your Web site.

Be smart—your Web site will be in a public space. As tempting as it may be to "borrow" a really neat photo, headline, or graphic from someone else's Web page—don't do it!

You may even surf around the Internet, and find an entirely new type of page, not even described in this book, that you would like to use. Go for it! There are very few rules on the Internet, and the few guidelines here in this book can be broken, especially if it means communicating your business message more clearly to your customers. You may even get ideas shopping around at your competitors' sites (which is fine, as long as you don't *plagiarize* directly from them—*i.e.*, take words, images, colors, or concepts directly from them). Remember, you know your customers the best. Even a *professional* Web designer can't know more about your customers and your business than you do.

Adding More Pages Later

Once you get your basic, five-page Web site published, you can, of course, add more pages later—as many as you'd like. Don't worry right now that you will be limited by the five-page standard. Adding pages is much easier than starting a new Web site, so once you have this mastered, it will be a piece of cake!

Warning!

Just be warned—creating Web sites is so fun and easy, and the results are so fast, that you just may find yourself cranking out page after page. It's wonderful to see such an attractive, interactive marketing piece of your very own out there. In fact, it's downright addictive. Don't say I didn't warn you!

Chapter 3

STEP 1: PURCHASE YOUR DOMAIN NAME

B elieve it or not, it only takes five easy steps to create a Web site. Yes, that's right—only five steps. And if you stick with the basic five pages, you can complete all those steps in a single day. That's right—one day! Not only that, but if you choose your Web host, domain name, and design software carefully, you can do it for less than $500. Don't believe it? Read on!

Buy Your Domain Name Now!

Buy your domain name now, even if you are unsure of whether you will ever use it. It is easier to buy it now, and let go if it later—rather than trying to buy a popular domain name that someone snapped up ahead of you.

The five easy steps to getting your Web site up and running are:

Step 1: Purchase your domain name.

Step 2: Write the Web content.

Step 3: Design the page layout.

Step 4: Find a Web host.

Step 5: Publish the Web site.

In order to make this as quick and painless as possible, I have made suggestions throughout each chapter to speed up the writing, design, and publication process. I have also suggested some of the most popular software, hosting, and domain services out there. Since you have already finished the planning and organizing stages, you are ready to begin!

What Is a Domain Name?

Total Time: 15 minutes

The first step to creating any Web site is to purchase the domain name. Even if you are only considering creating a Web site at a later date, this step is still absolutely critical to do immediately.

$ Total Cost: $5–$35 for one year. It may even be less if you purchase the domain along with a hosting plan, or in multiple-year packages.

Why? Because the best names sell out quickly, and you don't want to start a business, then discover later that you cannot own the domain name that you wanted.

But we're getting ahead of ourselves. Let's start at the beginning.

What Is a Domain Name?

Domain names are nothing mysterious. Don't let the techie title fool you. In fact, if you have *ever* visited a single Web site, you have seen a domain name.

The domain name is the address that you type into a Web browser to go directly to the Web site you want to see. For example, the following are domain names—and some of them may even be familiar to you:

» *www.amazon.com*
» *www.ebay.com*
» *www.yahoo.com*
» *www.msn.com*
» *www.peterswriting.com*

In fact, every Web site that you know and love started out one time, humbly, as nothing more than a simple domain name, without any content, graphics, or fancy Web design. And that's the same place where your Web site will begin, too.

The most common domain name extensions include:

» .com
» .org
» .biz
» .net

There are, however, many other variations that are growing in popularity, including:

» .us
» .name
» .info

Notice that in the example above, almost all the domain names have the same format. They start with *www.*, move on to the business name, and then finish up with *.com* (or *.biz, .net, .org*, etc.). You will want to follow the same format with your own domain name.

Purchase Your Very Own Domain Name

Luckily, buying a domain name is not like buying a car. You don't walk out of the lot with a shiny new vehicle, a sparkly set of keys, and a massive case of buyer's remorse. In fact, it may not feel like you are getting much of anything—you are simply buying a virtual intellectual property. There will be no real physical product exchanged, and most likely, you will never talk to a live person—you will conduct the entire purchase over the Internet!

But what you get will be very valuable to your business. Because this will be the start of the most important brochure you will ever create for your company: your Web site. In fact, buying a domain name has become almost as important as choosing a name for your business.

So where do you begin? Start with your business name.

Not All Domain Name Extensions Are Created Equal

Hands down, the best domain name extension for businesses is still .com. Why? Because customers will automatically look for a .com address when they are searching for you on the Internet. If it's at all possible to get a .com extension, do it.

Start with Your Business Name

The first, and best, option for you is to buy the domain name that is closest to your full and complete business name . . . and that uses the extension *.com* (unless you are an educational organization, where it's best to be *.edu*, or a nonprofit organization, where it's best to be *.org*). To find out if your business name is available as a domain name, you can do a quick search through one of the popular online domain name registration services. This step will take you less than five minutes.

For example, Karla Snider is a successful freelance graphic designer, and a good friend of mine. She runs a freelancing business called simply, Karla Snider Design. When she decided to put up a Web site awhile ago to display her portfolio to clients, she went directly to her business name, with the most common extension, and got: *www.karlasniderdesign.com*.

Now clients have no trouble finding her or samples of her work. They can look at all the logos, brochures, business stationery, and direct-mail pieces she's designed in the past.

Go to a computer, open up a Web browser, and type in one of the domain name registration sites listed in the sidebar. When you get to their Web site, you will find a search function that will allow you to find out if the domain name of your choice is available.

 ## Domain Name Registration Sites

Here are a few of the most popular places where you can register and purchase your domain name:

- » *www.networksolutions.com*
- » *www.register.com*
- » *www.godaddy.com*
- » *www.1cheapdomains.com*
- » *www.aplus.net*
- » *www.maddogdomains.com*

Enter your desired name and run a search. If it's available, you are in luck—purchase it directly on the domain registration site. Most will require a credit card or PayPal account.

Be aware that your domain name purchase is similar to a lease. You will purchase your name for a set length of time—such as one year, five years, or ten years. The cheapest way to start is by purchasing one year only; however, they may offer you a discount for purchasing multiple years or by purchasing the domain name in combination with a Web hosting plan. If the deal looks good, take it. (Read "Step 4: Find a Web Host" before you commit to a plan.) You will also likely be offered several other services, such as encryption, security, protection, etc. However, you are *not required* to purchase anything besides a domain name. And you are not required to purchase a domain name for longer than a year.

If you are planning to be in business for longer than a year, I strongly recommend purchasing your domain name for two years or more. You will get a good discount, but more importantly, if you forget to renew later, you won't run the risk of losing your domain name through expiration—which you'll dearly regret if you already have a Web site up and running!

 Warning!

Many domain name registration sites sell their domain names as part of a Web hosting or design package. Some even give them away for free. This is a standard marketing offer in the business, and may save you some money in the long run. However, don't sign up for more services than you want. You are not required to purchase anything besides a domain name from a domain name provider.

What If My First Choice Is Unavailable?

If your first choice of domain name is unavailable, you have a couple of options. You can try purchasing the same name with a different extension or you can try formulating the name in a different way.

For example, if your business name is Crazy Tulips, LLC, but *www .crazytulips.com* is already taken, your domain name registration site will probably suggest other alternatives for you to purchase. For example, the domain registration site may say:

Sorry, the domain name you are looking for is unavailable. Would you like to try:

www.crazytulips.org
www.crazytulips.net
www.crazytulips.biz
www.crazytulips.us

You are welcome to purchase one of those alternative options, and if that works for you, great. You are ready to buy. Move to the shopping cart and make your purchase. Once again, you will be offered many additional services, such as Web hosting, encryption, security, etc.; remember that you can—but you are not obligated to—buy them.

However, if you would rather get a .com site, because the .com extension is so prevalent and easy to remember, try "reformulating" the name to find a suitable match. In fact, your domain name Web site will likely suggest several options. See what comes up—you may be surprised. They may even suggest some good ones you had not considered.

For example, we come up with the following list of alternate names for Crazy Tulips:

> » *www.crazytulipsflowers.com*
> » *www.crazytulipschicago.com*
> » *www.crazytulipsforyou.com*
> » *www.crazytulipsbyjill.com*
> » *www.crazytulipsllc.com*

Remember, there is no rule that says that your domain name *must* match your business name exactly. In fact, many businesses wind up using a slight variation of their business name in their domain name. There are simply too many similar-sounding business names, making it impossible for everybody to use the same domain name. In our case, Peters Writing Services was just too darned long for a Web site ... *www.peterswritingservices. com* is quite a mouthful! So we purchased *www.peterswriting.com* instead— it's shorter, sleeker, and easier to remember.

Why Buy My Name as Soon as Possible?

Now back to our earlier situation. The reason it is important to buy your domain name as soon as possible—as soon as you read this book!—is that the best names sell out quickly. Even the oddest names can attract buyers, so don't assume that just because you have an unusual name, no one has purchased it. The best part is, you can do a quick search on most domain selling Web sites for free.

Let me give you an example. Let's say you started a business called Technology Associates. You repair computer equipment for home-based businesses. You are now ready to buy your domain name. What name should you purchase?

The obvious first choice would be *www.technologyassociates.com*. Let's take a look at one of the popular domain name registration sites and see if that name is free.

Hmmm. Unfortunately, *www.technologyassociates.com* is already taken. So is *www.technologyassociates.net*, *www.technologyassociates.org*, *www.technologyassociates.biz*, *www.technologyassociates.ws*, *www.technologyassociates.eu*, and *www.technologyassociates.co.uk*! That doesn't leave you a lot of options. About the best you can do at this point is take *www.technologyassociates.us* or *www.technologyassociates.info*. This could make it difficult for customers to find you easily.

Still Deciding on a Business Name?

If you are just starting your business, and you've already got a few business names in mind, spend a few minutes looking at the possible domain names online. Find out how many people (if any) are already using your name or a similar name. If you have narrowed it down to two or three choices, you may even want to buy all three domain names—just in case! This will prevent heartache later, and you can always let them expire.

Getting the right domain name is especially critical if you will be selling products exclusively online or will be using your Web site heavily later in your marketing efforts.

What If I Absolutely Must Have a Particular Domain Name, and the One I Want Is Unavailable?

If you make ginger candies, your business name is Ginger Candies, and you feel you absolutely *must* have *www.gingercandies.com*, but discover that it is already taken—then you still have a couple of options. You can:

> » Make a certified offer for the domain name.
> » Backorder the domain name.

What does it mean to make a certified offer for a domain name? In this case, you can make an instant, anonymous offer to buy the domain name from the person or business who owns it, using a third party acting as a broker. The third party is usually one of the domain registration Web site services. Check with your domain registration Web site to see if this is possible.

Keep in mind that the business who owns the domain name is not required to sell to you. You may or may not be successful with this approach, but if you are desperate, it is worth a try.

Not only that, but it isn't cheap. Many of them operate like an auction, where bids start at a minimum of $100, and can go as high as $25,000. Yikes! (But if you really have to have it—or your business success depends on it—it may be worthwhile to you.)

Clearinghouses for Expired and Deleted Domain Names

If you decide to backorder your domain name, here are a few Web sites that specialize in expired and deleted domain names:

» *www.snapnames.com*
» *www.dotcenter.com*
» *www.dots.org*

Most domain name registration Web sites also provide this service.

If you have the patience of a saint, backordering may be the way to go. There are clearinghouses that collect expired and deleted domain names. In fact, thousands of domain names are deleted or expire every single day.

The system is similar to that of making a certified offer—once the name expires, or is deleted, you have the opportunity to bid through the clearinghouse or domain registration service, which again acts as a broker. One bonus of these services: most don't require you to pay a penny until you actually receive the domain name that you want. And you can get notified as soon as the domain name is available.

 *Chapter 4*

STEP 2: WRITE THE WEB CONTENT

🕐 Total Time: 2 hours

Believe it or not, it's not all that difficult to write your own Web site content. You don't need to be a journalist or a professional writer to do it. In fact, I've had entrepreneurs in my seminars write a five-page Web site in as little as one hour (although two hours is probably more realistic).

§ Total Cost: $0

When you are writing the content for your Web site, only one rule applies: be brief, using the simplest language possible. Don't try to be fancy, or academic, or extra professional. Just describe your business and your service in a conversational tone. That not only makes it easier to read, but will also make it easier for you to write.

No Writing Experience?

Don't worry if you don't have any writing experience— or even a college degree. You can still write your own Web content. Web content is actually quite simple and straightforward to write. Just take a deep breath, get your pen working, and try the easy exercises in this section.

Writing the Pages for a Standard Five-Page Web Site

Let's start by writing the most common pages out there on the Internet: the pages for the standard, five-page Web site. I will give you step-by-step instructions for writing the content for the home page, services or products page, clients page, about us page, and contact us page.

Please note that you are not *required* to use all (or any of) these guidelines to write your Web site. You are welcome to be as creative as you want with your own.

Be Creative . . . But Don't Be Too Wordy

Be as creative as you want in writing your Web content—as long as you use no more than 350 words max per page. Any more than 350 words, and you risk losing your audience.

You'll want to stick to a guideline of roughly 250 to 350 words per page. Approximately 350 words is the absolute most you can squeeze onto a page; I prefer to stick to 250 words. Since very few people actually scroll down on a page, you don't want to be so wordy that no one reads your content.

The five pages we will cover in this section are:

» Home page
» Services/products page
» Clients page
» About us page
» Contact us page

Now let's look at the Web site map you created in Chapter 2, "Plan a Web Site for Your Business." If you did not do a site map and are just creating a standard five-page Web site, skip ahead to the writing instructions.

Are any of these standard five pages the same as what you have listed in your topic boxes? If so, check them off now. For example, most people have a home page on their Web site map. Go ahead and check off home page—and any of the other four standard pages—now.

Circle any remaining boxes that are *not* covered by the standard five-page Web site. For example, you may have a process page, a portfolio page, or a success stories page. For those unique pages, you'll find step-by-step content writing instructions for some of the most common of these in the section, "Common Additional Pages" on page 71.

Home Page

The home page is the most exciting page on your Web site. Why? Because this is the one page that everyone who stops by your Web site will see. This page will give your readers the skinny on exactly what you do in your business—in precisely four sentences.

Why only four sentences? Because a good home page should be short, sweet, and to the point. It should not be a detailed laundry list about your products, services, and history. Just like with a direct-mail postcard or brochure, you only want to whet your reader's appetite—not club him over the head with too much information. Save the details for the about us and product/service pages.

On the home page, you are going to write two paragraphs, of two sentences each, that give a nice, quick overview of your company. This overview should be able to be read in fifteen seconds or less. Remember, the goal of good marketing writing is to get someone interested enough in your company to learn more—and that's exactly what we do with a home page. We entice the prospective customer to click on other pages in your site—or call you.

There are four facts to communicate in the home page:

1. What your business specializes in
2. Who you service
3. How you help your clients (this is called a benefit statement)
4. Your promise to your clients

These four facts are the foundation for your home page. From these four simple facts, we will create four sentences; and these four sentences will become two paragraphs (that each have two sentences). Sound easy? Good.

Here's an example. Let's say your business is The Computer Whiz, and you fix computers. Your facts would look like this:

1. What your business specializes in: The Computer Whiz specializes in repairing home computers.
2. Who you service: The Computer Whiz services families and home-based businesses throughout the greater Raleigh area.
3. How you help your clients (benefit statement): The Computer Whiz rescues our clients from the hassles and stresses of failed, broken, or slow computers with our twenty-four-hour on-call service.

4.   Your promise to your clients: The Computer Whiz promise is to answer your phone call within sixty seconds, and be at your doorstep within sixty minutes—anywhere in Raleigh.

Notice how all the facts are written in complete sentences? Each one begins with the complete business name, and ends with a period. You'll want to do the same thing in your list of facts, too.

Use the Full Name of Your Business

Wherever possible, use the full name of your business when you are writing your pages—not initials. For example, I always use "Peters Writing Services"—never "PWS."

Even if your business name is long or cumbersome, it is better to repeat it. Why? Because your customer may only visit one page of your Web site—and you want to make sure that they know who you are, without a doubt. Even if it seems repetitive, it's the right thing to do.

Take out a pen and a blank sheet of lined paper, or use the space provided here. Write facts about your business.

1.   What your business specializes in:

_____

_____

_____

_____

2.   Who you service:

_____

_____

_____

_____

3.   How you help your clients (benefit statement):

_____

_____

_____

_____

4.   Your promise to your clients:

_____

_____

_____

_____

What Are Benefit Statements?

Benefit statements are simply facts about **how** you help your customers. The more specific you are, the more successful the benefit statement will be. Here are some examples of benefit statements:

» Save you money
» Reduce the amount of time spent on house chores
» Minimize the strain on your back
» Make you look sexier
» Improve your profitability
» Save time
» Reduce injuries on the job

The list of benefits used in Web writing goes on and on. To come up with your own, simply think of how you help your customers. Why are your services or products so important in their lives?

Once you have all four facts written, you can easily reassemble them into two paragraphs. First, string facts one and two together into one paragraph. Next, string facts three and four together into a second paragraph.

When we do that with our Computer Whiz example, we come out with this:

The Computer Whiz specializes in repairing home computers. The Computer Whiz services families and home-based businesses throughout the greater Raleigh area.

The Computer Whiz rescues our clients from the hassles and stresses of failed, broken, or slow computers with our twenty-four-hour on-call service. The Computer Whiz promise is to answer your phone call within sixty seconds, and be at your doorstep within sixty minutes—anywhere in Raleigh.

Now, it's your turn. String your first two facts together into one paragraph, then your second two facts into the next paragraph. Don't worry about how clunky it sounds right now with all those repetitive business names—we'll fix that later, in the next step.

Page Title: Home page

_____

_____

_____

_____

_____

_____

_____

Now we are ready to edit our text to make it flow more smoothly. The big problem we've got is that the business name is too repetitive. My guideline is to use a business name only once per paragraph. So, we will fix that in our next revision.

Why Do Edits?

Why bother editing the paragraph? Why not just write it correctly the first time? Because it is much more challenging to try to write something correctly the very first time. Even professional writers do one, two, and sometimes three drafts of content before they publish it to a Web site. On the first draft, they focus on content (getting the facts straight); on the next drafts, they focus on flow and style. The result looks much more polished, and reads more professionally.

You also need to read through for any other problem areas that need to be fixed, such as grammar, flow, or awkward phrasing. The easiest way to do that is to read it out loud—either to yourself or to a friend. As silly as it seems, I guarantee you that as soon as you read it out loud, you will hear the problems. Do the words flow smoothly? Does anything sound strange? Do you hear incorrect words, or grammar mistakes? Make notes on your above paragraphs.

After a few edits to our Computer Whiz paragraph, it now reads like this:

Home page

The Computer Whiz specializes in repairing home computers. We service families and home-based businesses throughout the greater Raleigh area.

At Computer Whiz, we rescue our clients from the hassles and stresses of failed, broken, or slow computers with our twenty-four-hour on-call service. Our promise is to answer your phone call within sixty seconds, and be at your doorstep within sixty minutes—anywhere in Raleigh.

Sounds a lot better, doesn't it? That's what a little editing will do for you!

Notice that our home page example use the word "we" instead of "they." This is standard writing format for Web page content. It builds intimacy for the reader, and subconsciously makes them feel like they are part of a casual conversation. Use "we" or "I" (first or second person voice) throughout the Web site, except for the about us page, where "he," "she," or "they" (third person voice) is more standard. (Don't worry about that now—you will read about third person voice later, when we write the about us page.)

Now, let's edit your home page. Take out your pen again, and rewrite it, this time with the changes we discussed.

Home page

_____

_____

_____

_____

_____

_____

_____

_____

When you are done revising, you are ready to include your home page text on your Web site. *Voilà!*

Products or Services Page

The products or services page is nothing more than a short description of your products, services, or both. If you mainly offer services to your customers, that's what you'll include here; but if you mainly offer products, that's what you'll include here. If you offer both, you should probably create a separate page for each—one for services, and one for products. Of course, you can try to list both on the same page, but this can be a bit messy—and awkward—with too much content in one small space.

Your goal on this page is to briefly communicate your services or products to your potential customers. And when I say briefly—I mean *briefly*. This is not a ten-page essay on why people should buy from you. This is a short, one-sentence overview of each product or service that you offer.

You may be saying, "Sure, I want to be brief, but I also want to tell my customers *everything* about my products. Shouldn't I give them as much information as possible?"

The answer is . . . *no*. Remember that a Web site is a piece of marketing literature, just like a Yellow Pages ad, a billboard, or a brochure. And the goal of any good marketing literature is to get someone to call you, drop by your store, visit your restaurant, or purchase something from you. All you need to do is whet their appetite—you don't have to give them the whole kit and caboodle.

Since we live in an age when people—especially customers—are bombarded by information from all directions, brevity is good. Brevity stands out. Because all you really want to do in a Web site is get people interested enough to make a phone call or try out a product or visit your new location.

The one exception here would be if you are setting up an online store. If you are planning to do that, give customers as much information as possible about the product so they can buy immediately. Check out Chapter 8, under the section titled "Online Stores" for more information on setting one up.

Why Be So Brief? Won't My Customers Want More Information?

One of the biggest mistakes that new business owners make is to give their customers too much information. It's better to give a brief overview—and encourage readers to get more information by calling you, or using a subpage—than it is to club them over the head with so much information that they lose interest. In marketing materials, being brief is the name of the game.

Your final product/services page will include a page title and a bullet list of between three and five products or services, each one followed by a one-line description. Sound easy? It is.

What If I Have More Than Five Products or Services?

If you have more than five products or services to list, you will probably need to create subpages, or separate pages. You could also group them into categories, which link to more detailed subpages.

For example, perhaps you are a gourmet food store and you have categories for showcasing your wine, cheese, chocolate, and fondue. You could set up each of these categories to lead to a separate subpage with the individual products listed for that category. The "Cheese" page would have a one-line description, then a hyperlink taking you to a subpage that includes descriptions of your Wisconsin Cheddar, Stilton, Baby Swiss, and Greek Feta.

If this is the case for you, strategize your effort. Consider kicking off your Web site with your favorite five products or services, then adding more later. This will get you up and running faster.

Now take out a pen, and get ready to write. Once again, you can either write your answers in the book, or on a separate sheet of paper.

Jot down the name of your top three (or up to five) products or services. After each item, write out the single most important fact about it. You do not need to use complete sentences or correct punctuation here. For example:

Products:

_____

» Wines: a fine selection of red and white wines, imported from Australia, Italy, France, and Chile
» Cheese: hard, soft, and semisoft cheeses from around the world, kept fresh in our top-of-the-line refrigerators
» Chocolate: more than 300 varieties of chocolate, for everyday or for holidays
» Fondue: sample our meat, cheese, and chocolate fondues every day in our store

It doesn't matter what facts you choose. Notice that we have not even used complete sentences. These are just notes on what is most important about these products for the customer. And that's all you have to do, too.

Now it's your turn. List between three and five of your favorite products or services, and a casual, one-line description of each. Don't forget to include your page name title at the top—whether it's products or services.

Products:

_____

_____

_____

_____

What If I Have Fewer Than Three Products or Services?

If you have only one or two products or services, you may wish to assign a page to each one, allowing you to add more detail. You could add up to four facts for each. You would then split them up into two paragraphs, just like you did on the home page. In fact, you could even call the page by the category—such as "Cheeses."

Now read over your list. You may find it helpful to read it out loud. Did you include everything you wanted to? Do your facts sound correct? If not, now is the time to revise, delete, and add.

When you are done, you are ready to include this page in your content.

Clients Page

The clients page is nothing more than a list of the customers you've done business with. If you are a business-to-business (B2B) company, your list will include business names; if you are a business-to-consumer (B2C) company, your list will include people's names.

Using Customer Testimonials

To make your clients page even better, ask your favorite customers for a testimonial quote. This is a one- or two-line quote, describing why they love your product or service. This goes a long way toward building credibility with your new customers.

You have a few options of how to present this list. You can present it as a straight list, lined up along the left-hand side of the page. You can present it as a bulleted list. You can present it in two or three columns. Or, you can group the customers on your list into categories—such as by industry (e.g., healthcare, telecommunications, banking), or by type of product user (e.g., mothers, grandmothers, aunts, best friends, babysitters ... e.g., "What grandmothers say about our products").

Getting Permission First

Please note that some people are definitely not comfortable with having their names in your marketing materials. You should take the extra step of getting your customers' permission before publishing their name on your Web site, just in case. This can be as simple as a short e-mail requesting their permission. You don't want to create a nasty surprise for an unsuspecting, happy customer when they look at your new Web site and find their name there—without their knowledge or consent!

The fastest way to do it is to just create a straight list, in a single column, lined up along the left-hand side of the page, and that's what we'll do here. Include a minimum of five customers in your list, but you can have as many as you want. Here is one page where it's okay to for a user to scroll through lots and lots of information. The more customers you include, the better!

So for this page, simply jot down the names of all the customers you have done business with. It's that easy. If you serve businesses, then include the business name of each of your customers, at a minimum. For example, if you are a B2B business, your list might look like this:

Clients

Food Equipment Storage Co.

Linda Hall Lighting

Big Joe's Pizza Delivery

Litchfield County School District

Precision Manufacturing

If you are a B2C company, list your customers' names and locations. That should be plenty to give you credibility. So, instead of the list of company names, you will set up your list like this:

Page Name Title: Clients

Jennifer Fletcher, Albuquerque, New Mexico

Nell Putnam-Farr, Polo, Illinois

Audrée DeLisle, Bantam, Connecticut

Vlad Palma, Williamstown, New Jersey

Aya Reiss, Detroit, Michigan

 ### Don't Invent Names!

I probably don't have to tell you that it is a bad idea to invent names of individuals or companies anywhere in your marketing materials. This is especially true on your Web site, where people can quickly and easily check up on your credentials. Believe me, it's not worth it. If you are really stuck for customer names, substitute a different page instead. You can always add a clients page later.

Now it's your turn. Take out your pen, and create your own list here:

Clients

_____

_____

_____

_____

_____

Remember, you are not limited to the space here. Try to include at least five, if you have them—but you can add as many as you'd like. If they don't fit, just create two columns and keep writing!

Congratulations! You are finished with your clients page. Now, you are ready to move on to the about us page.

What If I Don't Have Any Customers Yet?

If you don't have any customers yet, don't sweat it. You've got a few options. Try one of these ideas:

> Idea #1: Write out a four-sentence description of the type of customer your product or service would most benefit. Start out with: "Our gold-lined envelopes are perfect for . . . "

> Idea #2: Instead of doing a customer page, try doing a how-it-works page. On this page, you simply write out a four-sentence description of how your service process works.

> Idea #3: Swap out this page with another one suggested in the "Additional Pages" section.

> Idea #4: If you have vendors or partners already signed up to act as your suppliers, create a supplier page instead. List the names of your vendors, partners, or suppliers, and their logos if possible (with their permission, of course).

> Idea #5: Skip this page altogether, and trim your Web site down to four pages. It won't hurt the overall message or success of your site if you only have four pages.

Remember, you can always add this page later, when you build up a few customers.

About Us Page

There are many, many ways to tackle an about us page. To make it simpler and easier for you, I have developed a standardized, straightforward technique for writing the content. Of course, you are not limited to this format—and you are welcome to add as much information as you'd like, provided that it fits into the 350-word-maximum page format (preferably with at least two paragraphs, to visually break up the information you are presenting). But this technique will cover the critical information for this page.

When customers click on the about us page, what do they want to know? They want to know that your business is legitimate. They also want to know a little more about you and your business. The about us page gives you an opportunity to differentiate yourself—and to build intimacy with the many prospective customers who will be visiting your Web site.

This page will also consist of two paragraphs, made up of two sentences each—just like the home page. There are four key content points to communicate here:

1. The history of your business
2. Why you started the business
3. A unique fact about your business today
4. A philosophy statement

These four key content points will become the foundation for the whole page. They will translate into four sentences that will become the two paragraphs . . . that become the entire page. It's that simple.

Let me give you an example. Let's say your business is Healthy Bytz. You have been creating all-natural doggie treats for several years now. Your facts would look like this:

1. The history of your business: Healthy Bytz has been in business since 1997.
2. Why you started the business: Misty Bennett founded the company when she was dissatisfied with the filler-loaded doggie treats available at the store for her dog, Pearl; she believed that a healthier treat for dogs could be developed and enjoyed by pets at a reasonable price.
3. A unique fact about your business today: Healthy Bytz now produces 40,000 treats per year, sold in pet salons throughout the Southwest.
4. A philosophy statement: The Healthy Bytz team focuses on providing the highest quality, natural-ingredient treats available for dogs.

One more important thing to note here: about us pages are almost always written in the third person. What does that mean? That means that instead of using "we" or "I," you use "they," "he," or "she." This has become an industry standard in Web writing, and gives your content more credibility and authority for the reader. Even though you are the one writing it—and even though you used the more informal "we" and "I" in other areas of the Web site—that's okay. Trust me, as awkward as it feels, it's better to write this page in the third person.

Now, it's your turn. Take out your pen and jot down four facts about your business, in the same order we indicated above. Try using the third person "they," he," or "she."

1. The history of your business:

_____

_____

_____

_____

2. Why you started the business:

_____

_____

_____

3. A unique fact about your business today:

_____

_____

_____

4. A philosophy statement:

_____

_____

_____

What Facts Can I Include About My Business Today?

If you are looking for facts about your business today to include in fact #2, you don't have to look very far. In fact, there may be some right under your nose. Anything with a number in it is a good start. Try any one of these to jog your imagination:

» Number of customers serviced
» Different products you produce
» Number of widgets produced (total, or annual)
» Service lines you have available
» Years of experience
» People on your team

Once we have all the facts out in order, they can easily be reassembled into two paragraphs, with a little bit of editing. After stringing facts one and two together into the first paragraph, and then the next two facts into a second paragraph, we come up with this:

About Us

Healthy Bytz has been in business since 1997. Misty Bennett founded the company when she was dissatisfied with the filler-loaded doggie treats available at the store for her dog, Pearl; she believed that a healthier treat for dogs could be developed and enjoyed by pets at a reasonable price.

Healthy Bytz now produces 40,000 treats per year, sold in pet salons throughout the Southwest. The Healthy Bytz team focuses on providing the highest quality, natural-ingredient treats available for dogs.

It's your turn. Your next step is to string your facts together into two paragraphs. Try it here:

About Us

_____

Paragraph #1:

_____

_____

_____

Paragraph #2:

_____

_____

_____

Can you add more lines than this? Of course. If you have something else important to say about your company, do it. Just make sure you don't exceed the maximum of 350 words per page. You want to make sure your page is neat, tidy, and not overbearing.

Next, read the paragraph out loud. How does it sound to your ear? Is the grammar correct? Does the wording flow well from one sentence to the next?

You may want to make a few small editing tweaks so it sounds smoother. For example, after a few small edits to our Healthy Bytz paragraph, it now reads like this:

About Us

Healthy Bytz has been in business since 1997. Misty Bennett founded the company when she was dissatisfied with the filler-loaded doggie treats available at the store for her dog, Pearl. She believed that a healthier treat for dogs could be developed and enjoyed by pet owners at a reasonable price.

Today, Healthy Bytz produces 40,000 treats per year, sold in pet salons throughout the Southwest. Their team still focuses on providing the highest quality, natural-ingredient treats available for dogs.

Do the same thing with your own paragraphs. Read them out loud. Or better yet, show them to a friend or colleague. Are they written in third person? Do the facts flow smoothly? Make any minor edits or adjustments that you need to. If you'd prefer to rewrite it from scratch, go right ahead.

About Us

_____

_____

_____

_____

_____

_____

_____

_____

Congratulations! You've successfully tackled the toughest page of content in your Web site—the about us page. The rest is a piece of cake.

Contact Us Page

The easiest page to write on your Web site is your contact us page. The contact us page shares your critical contact information with your customers, so they can find you.

But the contact us page does more than that. It also shows prospective customers (who may never even meet you) that you have *credibility*. What does this mean? This means that customers want to know that you are a real, bona fide business—not some fly-by-night operation. And seeing bona fide contact information—with a real street address—is a part of that decision.

Some customers feel okay about doing business with a totally virtual company, one that has no physical address or phone number. But most prospective customers don't. They feel that if they can't find you, they can't trust you. Be sure to include all possible contact information in your contact us page—especially a mailing address.

(If you don't believe this, think about your own buying practices. Would you spend $500 with a mail-order catalog that wouldn't tell you where they were located? Neither would I.)

What If I Don't Want to List My Address?

What if your business is home-based, or is located at an address that you'd rather not publish? Then you have a few options. You can:

- » Get a P.O. box at a U.S. post office
- » List a suite number on your home address, to make it appear like an office (e.g. Suite 101)
- » Rent a virtual office space at a local office park
- » Rent a virtual address through a service (similar to a P.O. box, only privately owned)

But whatever you do, please be sure to list a legitimate address. Customers will not buy from you without one.

The information that you should on your contact us page includes:

- » Line #1: Company name and logo (if you have one)
- » Line #2: Phone number
- » Line #3: Physical address
- » Line #4: Mailing address (if different from your physical address)

You may also want to list some of the following optional information:

- » Line #5: Fax number for the company
- » Line #6: Contact person's name, title, direct phone number, and e-mail address
- » Line #7: Directions or map to your facility (critical if you are in retail, restaurant, or hotel industry)

Here is an example of a contact us page, written in order, with the above information included:

3 Women and a Truck Movers, Inc.

Phone (802) 555-4565

117 Revolution Rd.

Manchester Center, VT 05255

Fax (802) 555-4566

Rosalie Smith, Customer Service Manager, (802) 555-4565, x102 or *rosalie@3womenandatruck.com*

After that, just add a page title, and you're done. You can just call the page "contact us." As simple as it sounds, it's the name everyone is expecting—and they will know exactly what it means.

Now that you've seen the guidelines, you are ready to write your own contact us page.

Contact Us

Line #1: _____

Line #2: _____

Line #3: _____

Line #4: _____

Line #5: (optional) _____

Line #6: (optional) _____

Line #7: (optional) _____

Congratulations! You have finished writing the five standard pages for a Web site. Nice work!

If you are planning to create the standard five-page Web site in this book, you are finished writing the content. You are ready to move on to Step 3: Design the Page Layout.

However, if you had planned to create more pages, now is the time to go back and review your Web site map. Are there any boxes that you haven't written content for, boxes that you circled at the beginning of this chapter?

If so, you may find instructions for writing them in the next section, titled "Common Additional Pages in a Web Site." If you don't see the pages you'd like to create there, I've created a special technique for writing just about any page you can think of, in the section called "Writing Miscellaneous Pages from Your Site Map."

Common Additional Pages in a Web Site

Here are instructions for writing some of the most common additional pages in a Web site—beyond the standard five. These are the additional pages that we get requested to write most frequently from our customers.

How-It-Works Page

The how-it-works page is a short description of how the process works when the customer buys from you. This page works very well, especially for new businesses, no matter whether you are selling products or services. It answers the silent question in every prospective customer's head: "If I buy something from this company, *how will it work?* What can I expect to happen?"

This is nothing more than a simple, step-by-step description of the buying process, limited to about five steps. It describes exactly what the customer is required to do to engage the company's services, and exactly what the company does to fulfill the customer's needs, in a specific, concrete way.

You should strongly consider adding a how-it-works page if you are creating an online store, because your customer needs to understand the transaction process. This can save you many, many phone calls about your buying process, particularly in an expensive sale.

If you are a new business, or if you do not yet have enough customers to justify a clients page, the how-it-works page is an excellent substitute for a clients page. It builds confidence in your service process without having to see the other customers' names.

A how-it-works page includes about five steps that describe your service process. Let's say I am selling our classroom training services, a longtime service line at Peters Writing Services. Here is our service process, and here is what our how-it-works page might look:

How It Works

Step 1: We analyze your current training needs through observation and interview.

Step 2: We create a design document, outlining the recommended content and length of the class, including activities.

Step 3: We write a draft of the training materials for teacher and participant.

Step 4: You provide us with recommended changes to the materials.

Step 5: We facilitate a "dress rehearsal" of the class using the materials, and refine them as needed.

Now think about your own business. What is your typical sales and service process? Yours may be just as complex as this one. Or, it may be as simple as three steps. Here is another example, a sample process for a monogrammed stuffed animal service, geared toward kids:

How It Works

Step 1: You add your favorite stuffed animal to the shopping cart.

Step 2: We personalize your stuffed animal with a name, date, and special occasion.

Step 3: Your personalized stuffed animal arrives at your house within eight to ten business days.

It's your turn. For your how-it-works page, simply write down each step, using a complete sentence. You can even leave in the word "step," to make it clearer to your reader.

When you are done, read it out loud, or share it with a trusted colleague, and make any final edits that you see fit.

How It Works

Step #1: _____

Step #2: _____

Step #3: _____

Step #4: _____

Step #5: _____

Samples or Portfolios Page

If you are in a business that relies heavily on past performance, you will benefit greatly from including a page with samples, or a portfolio. It can use very little actual text—and be as simple as a series of pictures with title descriptions.

Businesses that do visual work, such as photography or architectural design, benefit the most from a samples page. Prospective customers must be able to see their past work visually; words simply cannot describe the power of their experience. If you are in the same situation, you'll definitely want to include a portfolio.

A few types of businesses that commonly use a sample or portfolio page:

- » Architects
- » Artists
- » Construction firms
- » Engineering firms
- » Graphic designers
- » House renovators
- » Landscape designers
- » Photographers
- » Writers

To create a samples or portfolios page, you will first need to complete your basic Web page design first (see next chapter, "Step 3: Design the Page Layout"). Once you have your basic Web page design completed, you will be ready to modify it to display your samples.

The easiest way I've found to display samples is to create a separate page layout for a portfolio, then line up the images, one right after the other. Just line them up vertically; customers can then scroll down to see the samples. A caption title describing each sample helps, too, and this can be done in a bold font. This page will need to be laid out individually, using your Web design software or your Web service provider.

If you are using photos of your work, make sure that they are at least 300 x 400 pixels in size, and look nice enough aesthetically to be included on your site. (For more information on photos, read the section on photos included in "Step 3: Design the Page Layout.")

One final note: you'll want to be sure to include at least three pictures, but there is no limit to how many you can have on your page. Less than three, and it looks too amateur. This is one of those exception pages where it's fine for people to scroll down to see more content, if necessary.

FAQs Page

"FAQs page" means "frequently asked questions" page. Why dedicate a page just to questions and answers? Because it helps to anticipate—and overcome—some of the lingering doubts in your customer's mind about buying from you. And it does so in a simple, easy-to-read format. Over the past few years, this has actually become an industry standard page, and most readers of your Web site will understand exactly what it is, as soon as they read it.

If you are planning to set up an online store, or if you are marketing a highly complex service through your Web site, an FAQs page may help reduce hesitation about buying from you. If you spend a lot of time during the sales process educating your customers on your services, or if you get a lot of questions on your products, an FAQs page may be right for you.

A typical FAQs page has between four and eight simple, one-line questions, each one followed by a simple answer, with between one and three sentences in the response. They are always written in complete sentences.

To start your own FAQs page, think about the kinds of questions that your customers often ask you during the sales process. (If you are a new business without customers, try to imagine the concerns your new customers might have.) They want to know: When will the product arrive at their doorstep? What if they have a return or exchange? How can they reach customer service? What is included in the maintenance package? These are exactly the kinds of questions your customers want answered *before* they buy from you.

Common FAQs Questions

Here are some common FAQs questions that you are welcome to modify to use in your own Web site:

» How do I return a product?
» Who do I call if I have a problem?
» What is included in this service package?
» How much does this service cost?
» What are the maintenance fees?
» Are there any hidden fees?
» What if I need an exchange?
» What if the product never arrives?

You can be as creative as you like in coming up with your questions. Just be sure to limit the length of each question to one sentence, and of each response to no more than three sentences (unless you have an important reason for doing so).

When you write an FAQs page, you always start off a question line with a "Q:" and an answer line with an "A:". That indicates quickly and clearly what information the customer needs to read. For example:

» Q: When will my custom-printed business cards arrive in the mail?
  A: Within three business days.

» Q: How do I choose the paper?
  A: By signing into your customer account, and clicking the "Paper" button.

When you write an FAQs page, you will always write the questions from the point of view of the customer. That is, you write them almost as if you were speaking for the customer, using words like "I," "my," "me," or "we." Then, you write the answers from your own point of view, as if you were literally answering the question.

Here's an example. Let's say that the Kennewick Book Store opens up in Olathe, Kansas. They sell used books. They receive too many phone calls with questions about how to buy and sell books at their store, so they decide to add an FAQs page to their Web site. Their goal is to see if that helps answer some of their customers' questions—*before* they lug a large box of books into the store.

Here is what their FAQs page looks like:

FAQs

Q: Do you accept credit cards?

A: *We accept all major credit cards, including Visa, MasterCard, American Express, and Discover.*

Q: Can I sell you my books?

A: *Yes. We pay cash for new and slightly used books only. We do not accept worn, torn, dusty, or overly used books.*

Q: How does the book-buying process work?

A: *You may schedule an appointment with us to review your books at any time on Mon. – Fri., 9:00 a.m. – 5:30 p.m. Call (913) 555-1200 to schedule an appointment.*

Q: How much do you pay for books?

A: *We pay $1.00 – $5.00 for books, depending on their age, quality, and rarity. We will give you an assessment of the value of your books when you arrive for your appointment.*

Q: Can I exchange my books for store credit?

A: *Yes. If you accept store credit instead of cash, you will receive BONUS double credit—we will pay $2.00 – $10.00 of in-store credit for the books, depending on age, quality, and rarity.*

Notice how the questions are written from the perspective of the customer, and answers are written from your perspective as the business owner. This is nothing fancy, just standard formatting for FAQs documents everywhere—whether it's on a Web site, a brochure, or a technical manual.

Now, it's your turn. Jot down a list of between four and eight questions that a customer might be thinking. Think about your product or service.

What questions do you typically get from your customers? This is a good place to start.

What If My FAQs Page Is More Than 350 Words?

Throughout this book, you will see references to the suggested limit of 350 words maximum per page. The Q&A page, however, is a different animal altogether. Customers expect to see more text on this page, and often don't mind scrolling down the page to learn more from this easy, back-and-forth format. Go ahead—use more than 350 words if you need to. It works fine on this particular page.

Next, jot down answers to the questions. Imagine yourself sitting down, having a cup of coffee with a customer who was interested in buying from you. What would they ask you? How would you respond to their questions? What would you say? That is the information you want to include here. Be sure to use complete sentences, and be sure to limit it to no more than three sentences in your answer.

FAQs

Q: _____

_____

A: _____

_____

_____

Q: _____

_____

A: _____

_____

_____

Q: _____

_____

A: _____

_____

_____

Q: _____

_____

A: _____

_____

_____

Q: _____

_____

A: _____

_____

_____

Q: _____

_____

A: _____

_____

_____

Success Stories Page

If you have solved a few customer problems already with your business, try including a success stories page. This simple page shares stories with your future customers about how helpful you've been to past customers. In fact, this can be even more impressive than a client list.

One great benefit of a good success story is that it educates your prospective customers in an intuitive way, using storytelling. After all, a success story is nothing more than a short story, describing the problem, the service or product that solved it, and how it benefited your customer overall. You can jam a lot of great information into a very small space, without giving your reader a "hard sell." In fact, a success story page has got so much information in it, it's like combining a how-it-works page, services/products page, and about us page—all rolled up into one.

But don't let that scare you into thinking that it's difficult to write. A success story is nothing more than a short, one-paragraph story that describes how you've helped a client in the past. Most good success stories can be written in about three sentences; that's what we'll do here. I also like to add a summary title to my paragraph, which creates a nice headline. With three good success stories, you've got a full page. (You can add more if you want, but probably no less than three to start.)

When you write your success story, you'll use complete sentences. You will also want to write about your business in the third person, using either the company name, "he," "she," or "they." Just like with the about us page, this style gives the story more credibility—and in fact, this style has also become an industry standard for writing testimonials and success stories.

Here are the four things you'll need to write your success story:

Fact #1: Summary of how your product or service helped the customer (not a complete sentence)

Fact #2: Customer names and description of their problem (complete sentence)

Fact #3: Description of your product or service, and how it solved the problem (complete sentence)

Fact #4: Benefit the customer now enjoys, thanks to your product or service (complete sentence)

Fact #1, which is a short, one-line summary, will become the title of your success story. This is the one fact you'll be writing that does *not* need to be a complete sentence.

Here's an example. Let's say that Green Acres Landscape has developed a specialty in fixing wet basements, especially during the rainy season.

They would like to show off this service better through a page of customer testimonials, and they have a recent example they'd like to use. Here are the facts they jot down:

Success Stories
Fact #1: Summary of how your product or service helped the customer (does not need to be a complete sentence): French drain solves wet basement problem

Fact #2: Customer names, and description of their problem (complete sentence): Shirley and Mark DeMeo were frustrated because their finished basement flooded with only one inch of rain, leaving their carpet, walls, and furniture soaked.

Fact #3: Description of your product or service, and how it solved the problem (complete sentence): Green Acres Landscape fixed the problem in two days by installing a 4" wide linear French drain across the back of the house.

Fact #4: Benefit the customer now enjoys, thanks to your product or service (complete sentence): Shirley and Mark now enjoy a dry basement every time it rains, without the expense of replacing ruined carpet and furniture.

Now, we can use the first summary fact as a nice headline, and string the rest of the facts together into one single paragraph. When we do that, it turns into a nice short story, like this:

Success Stories
French drain solves wet basement problem

Shirley and Mark DeMeo were frustrated because their finished basement flooded with only one inch of rain, leaving their carpet, walls, and furniture soaked. Green Acres Landscape fixed the problem in two days by installing a 4" wide linear French drain across the back side of the house. Shirley and Mark now enjoy a dry basement every time it rains, without the expense of replacing ruined carpet and furniture.

What Is a Headline?

A headline is a short, catchy line that can be used as a title for a paragraph, page, or section of a brochure. They are often used in the marketing world to attract attention or catch a reader's interest. I use headlines on my success stories to attract a potential client's attention.

Now, it's your turn. Think about a time when you helped a customer to solve a problem with your product or service. The bigger the problem, the juicier the story! Think of a doozy. When did you *really* help someone, and have a great impact on their life or their business?

Don't Make Up Your Success Story!

No matter how much you are tempted, please don't invent a success story. If you really can't think of a good success story, call a customer that you really like and ask them to suggest one. If you simply don't have enough customer experience yet, skip this page and try adding a how-it-works page instead.

When you have a good success story in mind, take the next step. Jot down your four key facts to the story. Remember to use complete sentences for your facts, *except* the first one (which will be used later as a headline). You will also want to use third person for your sentences—using the customer name, your business name, "he," "she," or "they."

Success Stories

1. Fact #1: Summary of how your product or service helped the customer (not a complete sentence):

_____

2. Fact #2: Customer names and description of their problem (complete sentence):

_____

_____

_____

3. Fact #3: Description of your product or service, and how it solved the problem (complete sentence):

_____

_____

_____

_____

4. Fact #4: Benefit the customer now enjoys, thanks to your product or service (complete sentence):

_____

_____

_____

 ## Do I Need Customer Permission to Use Their Success Story?

You are not required to get customer permission to use a success story about him or her—but you would be wise to do so. Why? Because occasionally, customers do not want their name (or company name) displayed on other people's marketing materials. Banks, security firms, and some technology firms are particularly fussy about this; some of the entrepreneurs who participate in my writing seminars have even discussed legal action from angry customers.

But don't let this scare you away from trying your hand at a success story page. A good success story page can help your business immensely. All you need to do is e-mail a client and ask for their permission to mention their story on your Web site. Let them know that it will help you out with marketing your business. When they write back to approve it, you will not only feel confident that they are okay with it, you will also have their approval in writing.

Once you have the facts jotted down, look them over. Are there any missing complete sentences—for example, are there periods missing at the ends of sentences? Are they written in third person? If they look good, you are ready to string them together into a headline and a paragraph.

Success Stories

_____

_____

_____

_____

_____

_____

When you are finished with your paragraph, you may want to edit it. Read it out loud, and listen to how it flows. If it sounds jagged in spots, change the wording. If there are grammar errors, fix them. Better yet, ask a friend or trusted colleague to read it for you, and give you feedback. If you disagree with their feedback, you can always ask another person to read it for you, too.

For a good success stories page, you really need at least three stories— from three different customers. You have a great start here, since you've already completed your first one. Now, you are ready to write a few more.

Here are the questions once again, plus additional space for you to write out your paragraphs. Good luck!

Success Stories
1. Fact #1: Summary of how your product or service helped the customer (not a complete sentence):

_____

2. Fact #2: Customer names, and description of their problem (complete sentence):

_____

_____

_____

_____

3. Fact #3: Description of your product or service, and how it solved the problem (complete sentence):

_____

_____

_____

_____

4. Fact #4: Benefit the customer now enjoys, thanks to your product or service (complete sentence):

_____

_____

Now, rewrite it into a complete paragraph:

Success Stories

_____

_____

_____

_____

_____

_____

Success Stories

1. Fact #1: Summary of how your product or service helped the customer (not a complete sentence):

_____

2. Fact #2: Customer names, and description of their problem (complete sentence):

_____

_____

_____

_____

3. Fact #3: Description of your product or service, and how it solved the problem (complete sentence):

_____

_____

_____

_____

4. Fact #4: Benefit the customer now enjoys, thanks to your product or service (complete sentence):

_____

_____

_____

_____

Now, rewrite it into a complete paragraph:

Success Stories

_____

_____

_____

_____

_____

_____

Testimonials Page

If you are an established business, a testimonials page is a great way to demonstrate the credibility of your business. Customer testimonials say that you are a real, bona fide business, and that other customers have worked with you and enjoyed it. It can do wonders for your sales, especially if you are selling directly over the Internet.

The key to a successful testimonials page is:

> » Include as many testimonials as you can (with a bare minimum of three).
> » Include as much information as you can about the customer (including, if possible, their name, title and business, or city and state).

A testimonial only needs to be one line long, but it can be as long as four or five lines. A good testimonial comes from a happy customer who has good things to say about your product or service.

If you've been in business for awhile, you may already have a few customer testimonials collected. Great! All you need to do is edit them down (if they are too long) to be two or three sentences, and post them on your Web page.

If you don't have any customer testimonials yet but want to include a testimonials page on your Web site, start actively soliciting them. This is how you do it: As soon as you've concluded a sale with a satisfied customer, ask them if they would be willing to write you a line or two, describing what they liked about your service. Or better yet, if they've complimented you verbally, jot it down on the spot and ask them if you could please include that positive comment on your Web site.

While not everyone is willing to do it, if you ask enough people, you should be able to collect four or five good ones to include on your Web site. Don't forget to ask them for permission to include their comments on your Web site (or in other marketing materials).

My business, Peters Writing Services, writes a lot of government proposals for smaller service and manufacturing businesses (typically with fewer than 100 employees) that want to win government business, but can't afford a full-time technical writer. Here is an example of a customer testimonial we included on our Web site for Peters Writing Services, taken several years ago from one of my favorite customers:

"We were very, very pleased by the high quality of Peters Writing's work on our government proposal. They were very professional, and did a great job working for us. We enjoyed working with them."

—Mary Janiak, President, Accent Controls, Inc.

This is the standard format I use for almost all the customer testimonials that we write—both for myself and for our customers. We use quotation marks, include a testimonial with between one and three sentences, and then list the customer's name, title, and business. In this case, Mary is not only the president, she's the owner, which makes it an especially good quote.

If you are including a consumer testimonial for a B2C business, you'll want to include the customer's name, city, and state of residence. Here is an example of a testimonial for a flower shop:

"Your flowers at my daughter's wedding this April were amazing. The lilies, berries, and feathers were so beautiful. Thank you for making our day so special."

—Mrs. Sarah Goodbody, Edmonton, Kentucky

Now, it's your turn. Start with a minimum of three testimonials—but you could have as many as eight or ten, or more. Use the same format I outlined above:

» A quote, using actual quotation marks
» The full name of the customer
» The city and state of the customer (if individual consumer) or the job title and company name of the

customer (if business)

Testimonials

"
_____

_____

_____

_____

_____ "

— _____, _____, _____
    (Name)   (Title OR City)   (Company OR State)

"
_____

_____

_____

_____

_____ "

— _____, _____, _____
    (Name)   (Title OR City)   (Company OR State)

"
_____

_____

_____

_____

_____ "

— _____, _____, _____
    (Name)   (Title OR City)   (Company OR State)

"_____

_____

_____

_____

_____

."_____

— _____, _____, _____
    (Name)   (Title OR City)   (Company OR State)

"_____

_____

_____

_____

_____."

— _____, _____, _____
    (Name)   (Title OR City)   (Company OR State)

"_____

_____

_____

_____

_____."

— _____, _____, _____
    (Name)   (Title OR City)   (Company OR State)

"

_____

_____

_____

_____

_____ ."

— _____, _____, _____
     (Name)   (Title OR City)   (Company OR State)

Bio Page

If you or your staff possess a tremendous amount of industry experience, or you have personal experience that you feel helps to sell your products or services, consider adding a bio page. A bio (short for "biography") page shares the professional, educational, and/or military background of the key individuals at the company. It can build great trust and credibility in the employees of the company, especially when personal service and expertise are critical to the sale, and are most commonly found on Web sites that sell services.

A bio page should have one—but no more than ten—bios of key staff members. These could include any (or all) of the following:

> » The business owner
> » Executives
> » Managers
> » Customer service personnel
> » Key talent (such as graphic designers, star lawyers, architects, doctors, etc.)
> » The whole team (if small enough)

These are instructions for a common format for Web bios. A good bio consists of three solid paragraphs, with about two sentences each. This usually ends up being about six facts. Of course, you can have more facts than that; I have been hired to write bios that are two pages long, and contain as many as thirty or forty facts. I have also seen effective bios that run a scant three sentences. However, a good bio can usually be captured in six solid sentences. The standard format that I suggest here works well in a Web format, as well as for a print brochure.

Here are the six facts you need to include in your bio:

Fact #1: A summary of your total experience

Fact #2: A statement about what you specialize in

Fact #3: Who you have worked with in the past (either employers or clients)

Fact #4: Your education, military, or applicable business experience

Fact #5: Any important memberships, associations, achievements, or awards

Fact #6: An optional personal line, discussing your volunteer work, hobbies, personal interests, family, or region where you live

Good Information for a Bio

While the guidelines I've given here for you are easy to use, you don't have to follow them. Feel free to be as creative as you wish. As long as it includes the following information, you should be safe:

- » Years of industry experience
- » Past clients or employers
- » Career specialty
- » Awards
- » Achievements
- » Association memberships
- » Education degrees/military experience
- » Personal hobbies or family information (optional)

Of course, you can tailor this format to suit your needs, and capture any particular experience or background information that you think is important to your customers. Remember, a bio is nothing more than another marketing tool; it just advertises your people, instead of your products.

Recycle Your Bios!

Bios can be used in lots of different formats. Once you have completed yours, feel free to recycle them in brochures, press releases, PowerPoint presentations, or any other marketing materials.

If you write this down line for line, you will have a total of six sentences. If you split these six sentences into three short paragraphs, you have a perfect bio for the Web—or any of your other marketing materials. Add your full name and title, and you are done. (If you are including more than one bio on your page, be sure to include full name and title of each person, as a way to introduce each bio separately.) You can even put the name and title in a larger, bold font, to attract attention, and set it off from the rest of the text.

Let's take a look at an example. Perhaps we have a senior tax accountant who is getting ready to launch her own business. Since she will be the only person in the business for the moment, her bio page only needs to include her own bio. Using the format outlined above, we come up with the following facts, making sure to put each one into a complete sentence:

Bio

Your Name & Title: Sahil Rajnikant, Senior Tax Accountant

Fact #1: A summary of your total experience: Sahil Rajnikant, CPA, has spent more than eighteen years as a tax accountant.

Fact #2: A statement about what you specialize in: Sahil Rajnikant specializes in preparing individual and business tax returns.

Fact #3: Who you have worked with in the past (either employers or clients): Sahil Rajnikant has previously worked as a senior tax accountant at four different firms, including Brown & Crouppen, Land/Air Express, Clear Talk Communications, and the McGilley Bros. Funeral Company.

Fact #4: Your education, military, or applicable business experience: Sahil Rajnikant received her bachelor of science in accounting at Loyola Marymount in California, and her MSA in finance at DePaul University in Illinois.

Fact #5: Any important memberships, associations, achievements, or awards: Sahil Rajnikant is a member of the American Institute of Certified Public Accountants, and was selected by Land/Air Express as the 2008 "Employee of the Year" for identifying over $100,000 in annual cost savings through the implementation of new tax strategies.

Fact #6: An optional personal line, discussing your volunteer work, hobbies, personal interests, family, or region where you live: Sahil Rajnikant enjoys boating, skiing, and attending the baseball games of her two children, Neil and Emily.

Notice that the facts of Sahil's bio are written in the third person. This is standard bio format, and you should do the same.

Taking Sahil's six facts, we are now ready to turn them into three short paragraphs. Pulling them all together, we get this:

Bio
Sahil Rajnikant, Senior Tax Accountant

Sahil Rajnikant, CPA, has spent more than eighteen years as a tax accountant. Sahil Rajnikant specializes in preparing individual and business tax returns.

Sahil Rajnikant has previously worked as a senior tax accountant at four different firms, including Brown & Crouppen, Land/Air Express, Clear Talk Communications, and the McGilley Bros. Funeral Company. Sahil Rajnikant received her bachelor of science in accounting at Loyola Marymount in California, and her MSA in finance at DePaul University in Illinois.

Sahil Rajnikant is a member of the American Institute of Certified Public Accountants, and was selected by Land/Air Express as the 2008 "Employee of the Year" for identifying over $100,000 in annual cost savings through the implementation of new tax strategies. Sahil Rajnikant enjoys boating, skiing, and attending the baseball games of her two children, Neil and Emily.

Of course, there is one big problem with this bio: it repeats Sahil's name way too much. It just doesn't sound right. To make this flow better, we need to solve this problem.

To do this, I use a device that I like to call a *repeater*. This is a simple writing device that allows you to repeat Sahil's name every so often, without tiring (or confusing) the reader. It may look complicated, but actually it is so standard in bios that readers will automatically process it when they see it.

This is how it works: the very first time a name is used in a bio, we write the full name—*Sahil Rajnikant*. The next time we write that name in the same paragraph, we use *she*.

In the second paragraph, we start with the repeater. This can be either *Sahil*, or *Ms. Rajnikant*—either one works fine. In our case, we'll use the more formal *Ms. Rajnikant*. After that, we flip back to *she*. The next time it's *Ms. Rajnikant*; then it's she . . . you get the picture.

Here's what it looks like now, edited with the repeater wording:

Bio
Sahil Rajnikant, Senior Tax Accountant

Sahil Rajnikant, CPA, has spent more than eighteen years as a tax accountant. She specializes in preparing individual and business tax returns.

Ms. Rajnikant has previously worked as a senior tax accountant at five different firms, including Brown & Crouppen, Land/Air Express, Clear Talk Communications, and the McGilley Bros. Funeral Company. She received her bachelor of science in accounting at Loyola Marymount in California, and her MSA in finance at DePaul University in Illinois.

Ms. Rajnikant is a member of the American Institute of Certified Public Accountants, and was selected by Land/Air Express as the 2008 "Employee of the Year" for identifying over $100,000 in annual cost savings through the implementation of new tax strategies. She enjoys boating, skiing, and attending the baseball games of her two children, Neil and Emily.

Doesn't that sound a whole lot better? And all we changed was a few simple words. A few words can mean a lot on a short Web page.

To summarize, here are some general guidelines for repeaters when writing a bio:

1. Use the full name in the title and the first time it is written in the bio (Sahil Rajnikant).
2. Use a shortened form of the name the first time it is written in each successive paragraph (Ms. Rajnikant).
3. Use "he" or "she" the second and third time it appears in any paragraph.

Should I Use the First Name or the Last Name as a Repeater?

Some people prefer to use the first name (Sahil) as a repeater. Some people prefer to use the last name (Ms. Rajnikant, Dr. Newcomb) as a repeater. There is no right or wrong answer; the choice is yours. Keep in mind that using the last name is generally more formal, and used in more conservative professions. It can also be used by anyone who wants to lend their name an extra "air of authority." Using the first name can give just the opposite effect, by making the person or business appear more casual. This works very well for businesses that want to build a fun atmosphere, or create close personal relationships.

Now, it's your turn. Start with your facts, then turn them into paragraphs. Remember, you'll want a minimum of one bio on a bio page, but you can have as many as ten, if you wish. If you have more than ten, it becomes cumbersome, unless you have a very good reason for it.

Jot down your facts here:

Bio

Your Name & Title:

_____

Fact #1: A summary of your total experience:

_____

_____

_____

_____

Fact #2: A statement about what you specialize in:

_____

_____

_____

_____

Fact #3: Who you have worked with in the past (either employers or clients):

_____

_____

_____

_____

Fact #4: Your education, military, or applicable business experience:

_____

_____

_____

_____

Fact #5: Any important memberships, associations, achievements, or awards:

_____

_____

_____

_____

Fact #6: An optional personal line, discussing your volunteer work, hobbies, personal interests, family, or region where you live:

_____

_____

_____

_____

What If I Don't Have a Title?

If you own the business, but don't yet have a title, choose one from the list of common ones, below—or make up your own. I have seen some very creative titles over the years, including Queen Bee, Head Ferret, Top Dog. However, keep in mind that if you are working in a very conservative field, a creative moniker may work against you!

» President
» Chief Executive Officer (CEO)
» Chief Operating Officer (COO)
» Owner
» Founder
» Sales Executive
» Customer Service Manager
» Account Manager
» Specialist (e.g., Writing Specialist)
» Senior (e.g., Senior Technical Writer)

After all, you are running the show. It's your business, and it's your title!

When you have your six facts written down, you are ready to string them together into three paragraphs. For your first draft, just put your six facts together into three paragraphs—facts one and two, then three and four, then five and six. It's that easy. Don't worry about editing, or getting the repeaters right—you can do that in the next draft:

Bio

Your Name & Title:

_____

Paragraph #1:

_____

_____

_____

_____

_____

Paragraph #2:

_____

_____

_____

_____

_____

_____

Paragraph #3:

_____

_____

_____

_____

_____

Now that you have a draft of your bio written, look for the following:

» Are your sentences written in third person (using your name, he, or she)?
» Are you using complete sentences (with appropriate punctuation at the end of each one)?
» Do you use the appropriate repeaters for names?

If you are missing any of these pieces, edit it now, or write a new draft below. This is an opportunity to also make any other edits that you feel are necessary—such as awkward phrasing, incorrect grammar, or misspelled words. Or, if everything looks good, you are done. Simply start over to add more bios, or move to the next Web page on your site map.

Bio
Your Name & Title:

Writing Miscellaneous Pages from Your Site Map

After writing the content for the five standard pages in a Web site and working through the common additional pages listed above, you may find that you still have not covered all the pages in your Web site map. That's okay. The good news is that most Web site content is fairly simple to write. Most of them follow the same basic formula: four facts or sentences, converted into two paragraphs—just like you did with the home page (with no more than 350 words per page). You can even use a bullet list format, if you choose.

At this point, you may be realizing (with a groan) that you have more pages on your site map than you really care to write. Those ten or twenty pages that you sketched out on your site map may have *seemed* like a good idea, at the time. However, you may not have the time (or energy) to write that many pages. That's okay, too.

If that's the case for you, don't be shy about scaling back your site map. There is nothing wrong with leaving a few pages for the future—or deleting them altogether. This happens constantly in a Web design project. Remember, as long as you can get your first five pages up and running, you're well on your way.

If you feel you still need to write a few of those miscellaneous pages that weren't included in the standard five-page Web site or the common additional pages, these instructions will help you do that. Once again, feel free to be as creative as you wish in writing this content. You know from your past exercises that every page of your Web site should include:

> » Page name title
> » 4 facts/sentences = 2 paragraphs of content

Let's start with your page title. You can simply use the page title you listed in the box on your site map.

Next, you are going to write four facts about your page topic, which will come out as four complete sentences. Later, you will combine these sentences into two paragraphs (each with two sentences).

To start, think about the topic you listed in the box on your Web site map. What is important for your customers to know about this topic? Is it related to your products or services? Or is it related to your customer service? Is it about your company, or your philosophy?

Whatever your topic is, think about it for thirty seconds—really think about it—and what your customers need to know about it. Once you have an idea in mind of what you want to communicate, you can start writing. Just pick any four facts at this point and jot them down. Order is irrelevant. But to be as efficient as possible, write them in complete sentences:

Page Title:

_____

Fact #1:

_____

_____

_____

Fact #2:

_____

_____

_____

Fact #3:

_____

_____

_____

Fact #4:

_____

_____

_____

Are you allowed to add more than four facts? Of course. If you come up with some really exciting things you want to tell your customers about, you can include as many as eight. But I would not exceed eight facts—any more, and you are at risk of losing your reader. People get bored and move on. If you want to include more than eight facts, add a separate page to your Web site.

Now look back over your facts. Read them out loud, if that helps you to visualize how they will sound to your customer. Make any revisions that you feel are necessary, after seeing them all together. If you see any facts that are not complete sentences, now is the time to fix them. Make sure they start with a capital letter and end with a period.

When you feel good about your facts, you are ready to string them together into paragraphs. Your goal is to come up with two paragraphs of two sentences each.

Start first with the one fact on your list that seems most exciting to your customers. Which one stands out for you? Which one grabs your attention? Whichever one you choose, circle it now. This will be your introductory sentence.

Why Can This Page Be Written in Any Order?

The fun thing about writing marketing materials—including Web sites—is that the structure is loose and simple. Many things are acceptable in marketing writing that are not acceptable in other writing, such as academics and business writing. The rules are much more relaxed.

The next time you look at an ad in a magazine, or watch a commercial on TV, pay attention to the way the information is presented. You will find that it is often not presented in any order! So don't worry about writing perfectly—just get the ideas out on paper. You can always edit them later.

Once you get the introductory sentence down, the rest of the facts can be included in any order. (Yes, I said *any order!*) Just add one fact after your introductory sentence to complete that paragraph, then move on to the next paragraph, and add your next two facts. You can edit them later.

Page Title:

_____

Paragraph #1:

_____

_____

_____

_____

_____

Paragraph #2:

_____

_____

_____

_____

Once you have completed this task, read the two paragraphs out loud. How do they sound to your ear? If they sound good, leave them as is— they are ready for publishing.

If they sound "wrong," or like they could use some rearranging, try them in a different order. Or make some changes to the wording. Take out any repetitions. Fix any grammar errors.

Try again here, with your edited version:

Page Title:

_____

Paragraph #1:

_____

_____

_____

_____

Paragraph #2:

Now, read it aloud again. Does that sound better? If so, your page is ready to be published.

Remember, marketing verbiage does not have to be perfect. It does not have to read like a Ph.D. thesis. It just needs to communicate your key messages. And to do that, it must be clear, simple, and full of facts. It doesn't really matter what order the facts are in—in the end, it's more important to communicate the *right content*, rather than the *perfect message*, to your reader.

Chapter 5

STEP 3: DESIGN THE PAGE LAYOUT

There are an endless number of ways you can design a page layout for a Web site. No doubt about it, there are as many variations to page designs as there are Web sites in existence today—literally millions.

But don't let this scare you. Your Web site does not need to be a masterpiece in design; nor does it need to follow any grand scheme for artistic vision. All you need to do is to lay out your company name, logo (if you have one), text, and navigation menus in such a way that it's easy for your readers to peruse—and to buy.

§ Total Cost: $15 – $400 (depending on which Web design tool you choose—and whether you use a Web design software or an online Web design package).

To make this as easy as possible, you can design one page layout—and one page layout only. After you have designed the single page layout, you will then incorporate all the text you have written into that same page design, to create all five (or however many) pages for your Web site. By using the same page design on all five pages of your Web site, you will not only streamline the design process tremendously, you will also make your life a whole lot easier. A single Web page design that is consistent from page to page will be visually more pleasing for your reader, too.

🕐 Total Time: 2 hours (if using the standard five-page Web site).

Here is the approach we will take to do your page design:

Step 1: Choose your Web design tool.

Step 2: Create your page layout.

Step 3: Add the content to the layout to create each of the pages of your Web site.

To make this even easier, I recommend that you start with a simple, standard page format. This standard Web page format has become quite common in the industry. It is easy, requires very little design experience to create, and is the equivalent of assembling wooden building blocks, because it uses squares and rectangles laid on top of one another. An advantage to this basic design is that you can be as creative—or as simple—as you like: you can leave it pretty much as is, or you can "dress it up" with your own style, incorporating pictures, new design elements, alternate navigation menus, etc. The choice is yours. But no matter how experimental you get with your design, you can always come back to this basic page template—simple, elegant, informative.

 Extra Functions to Consider

If you are planning to purchase a Web design software or use an online Web hosting package, consider any special functions that you might want in the future—and purchase one that includes these. Are you considering creating an online store? Have you thought about starting a blog? Is a podcast in your future?

Even if you are only considering adding one of these functions, it's still a good idea to make sure your software or service provider offers them. You don't have to purchase the services upfront, but you will know that they are always there if you need them. And if you do decide to use them, you'll be glad you did it—it will save you a lot of time and effort scrambling later for a plug-in solution.

Choose Your Web Design Tool

Before you can start doing any kind of design, choose a Web design tool to work with. If you are using a computer that already has a Web design software on it, such as the Mac computer from Apple, check that out first. In fact, many standard computer software packages now come with Web design software already included, or graphic design software that can perform Web design functions. Before you pull out the credit card, check out your own computer—you may be surprised to realize that you already have what you need!

If you don't already have a graphic or Web design software included on your computer, you will need to make a decision. You have two choices:

1. Web design software that works on your computer.
2. Online Web design packages offered through the Internet.

There are a few key differences between these two options. In general, the Web design software will be more expensive, but will offer you more flexibility in creating your page design. It will also require a bit of learning time.

The online Web design packages that you can buy over the Internet will be easier, cheaper, and faster to use. However, you will likely be limited to using pre-existing templates provided by the Web hosting service. You may also be required to buy a hosting plan as part of the deal, but these are, hands-down, the fastest way to get up and running, as everything is included in the service.

That's the basic scoop on the two choices; however, some additional discussion may help.

 ## Software "Wizards"

Most graphic and Web design software packages now offer "wizards" that walk you through a basic Web page design. A wizard should offer several options for page background, header, footer, navigation menus, body text, and titles. You can choose from preselected template options, or create your own. By using the wizard, you will save time—and get an education in how to put together a basic page layout.

Web Design Software

If you are looking for maximum creative control in your Web page design, and prefer to start with a blank page, consider an outright purchase of a Web design software package for your computer. While it may require a small time investment to figure out how to use it, the software in general is getting easier and easier to use. And even if it costs a little more money than an online package, in the long run, you will retain more control over your Web site design. Using your own software basically allows you the maximum creativity in designing your Web page.

You can buy a Web design software online or in a computer store, like Circuit City or Best Buy. If you spend some time browsing in the store or on the Internet, you will quickly get an idea of the different features and options available on each.

Be aware that prices vary tremendously on Web design software packages. Software packages start as low as $25 and run as high as $1,000, so comparison shop and find the best buy for your budget. In general, the higher the price of the software, the more sophisticated the features—and the more difficult it will be for a beginner to use. Also, be aware that much of the Web design software is tailored for "experts"—i.e., professionals who do this for a living. If you are a novice, stick to the simpler packages, or better yet—use an online Web design package.

If you have a background in graphics, or strong opinions about how the graphics on your Web site should look, you may enjoy the additional control offered by some of these packages. Otherwise, use one of the Web design packages you can get through Web hosts, which contain lots of predesigned templates where you just plug in your content, and then publish it.

If you decide to purchase a software, some of the features to look for include:

» Design wizards
» Stock photography
» Page templates
» Variety of navigation menus
» Miscellaneous design images

There are now a few Web design software programs that retail for less than $50 (unlike a few years back, when it was difficult to find anything less than $100).

Some of the more popular packages include (for a variety of prices):

» Web Easy Professional (Avanquest)
» iWeb (Apple)
» Web Express (MicroVision Development)
» Total Website Creator 3 in 1 (Cosmi)
» WebPage Designer GOLD (Boomerang Software)

» Instant Web Page (Upperspace)
» Interactive Web Editor (SJ Namo)
» Do It Yourself Website (INTELLYWEB)
» Web Page Construction Kit (Pearson Software)
» Expression Web (Microsoft)
» Web Page Construction Kit Deluxe (Macmillan)
» Contribute (Adobe)

Mac vs. PC

If you are using a Mac, make sure you purchase the appropriate software—you don't want to end up buying a software that is restricted only to PC, and vice-versa. Most software is nonreturnable once it is opened.

New software is coming out all the time. Also, the current software is always changing and getting better. Some companies—like Adobe and Microsoft—are going through tremendous changes with their graphic and Web design software, so the technology (and ease of use) is constantly evolving. Take a few minutes to do your own research—either at the store or online. Compare features and options. Look at the minimum requirements for computer capacity; think about your own skills with the computer. Then make the decision that's right for you.

Using Online Web Design Packages

Online Web design packages are perfect for you if you want to make this process as easy as possible. If you are in a hurry, have a very tight budget, are nervous about designing your own pages well, or just want a quick page design that looks snazzy and professional without spending a lot of time monkeying around on the computer, I recommend using an online Web design package.

Today, many Web hosting companies offer an easy, do-it-yourself Web design package that comes complete with their hosting services (an important and necessary step later, during publication—see "Step 4: Find a Web Host"). Basically, the Web design package includes hundreds of professionally designed page templates; you just plug in your content and set up your navigation menu, and you are done. These packages are quick, affordable, and easy-to-use, but limit the amount creativity you can have in your page design. You may also be locked into their hosting plans for a certain period of time.

How it works is this: rather than going to a computer store and buying a Web design software package, you will instead sign up for a Web hosting service, complete with a design package, through the company's Web site. The Web site then walks you through a step-by-step process of designing your Web page using their templates, and adding your content. You register for a hosting plan. Then, when you are ready, they publish the site for you. In fact, some of them can even take care of additional things—like registering your domain name, and setting up e-mail—for you.

The bottom line is: read the fine print on what you are committing to if you choose such a plan. Be sure that it is right for you. Look at some of their samples before you buy. Then you'll know you made the right choice.

 ## What Services Do Online Web Design Packages Offer?

Online Web design packages now offer tons of great options and services—all at the click of a mouse. Depending on the company, many of them now offer:

- » Domain registration
- » Hosting plans
- » Web marketing
- » E-mail accounts
- » Blog capability
- » Podcast capability
- » Online store hosting

If you are considering creating blogs, podcasts, or online stores later, for example, make sure to choose a provider that offers this capability. It will make your life much easier in the long run.

Keep in mind that new and better online Web design packages are popping up all the time—some competing on price, service, or number of templates to choose from. Here are a few that are popular today:

- » *www.godaddy.com*
- » *www.register.com*
- » *www.smallbusiness2day.com*
- » *www.fatcow.com*
- » *www.1and1.com*
- » *www.trendyflash.com*
- » *www.networksolutions.com*
- » *www.web.com*
- » *www.pages.com*
- » *www.homestead.com*
- » *www.sitecube.com*
- » *www.buildyoursite.com*

Creating Your Page Layout

One of the advantages of creating a simple page layout is that you can use it for all your Web pages—including the home page, the products or services page, the clients page, the about us page, and the contact us page. In fact, once you have the basic page layout designed, all you need to do is add the text that you've already written for each page of your site, and your Web site is designed and ready to publish.

Imagine that your Web site page is a simple box. There is a top side, left side, right side, and a bottom. We are going to keep this as simple as possible by working within a square design. This will make it easier for you to add, subtract, and move design elements as you go.

Work within the individual software or design package you have purchased to create your basic page layout. Each software or package should include instructions, wizards, or basic design elements for you to borrow from. It should also include a "Help" page or file to give you instructions in how to perform the basic functions that you will be adding here—we are not doing anything fancy. Check out whatever "Help" resources your tool includes before you get started.

The basic Web page layout includes the following items:

- » Top border
- » Logo
- » Left border
- » Navigation menu

» Page title
» Page text
» Copyright statement

If you stick to these basic page design elements, you can't go wrong. You can't include much less; without one of these items, you will be missing a major piece of your page. However, you can definitely add more to this—such as pictures, images, additional subtitles, additional borders, etc.

Do I Have to Have a Logo?

A logo has become such a standard part of Web design that it is strongly recommended. A logo shows that you are serious about your business; it can easily be created by you, or commissioned through a good graphic designer. (For advice on logos, see my book, The Ultimate Marketing Toolkit.) But if you do not have a logo, don't despair. You may wish to substitute a photo, shape, image, or other design element in the upper-left corner of the Web page.

Here is a template for a standard page layout that includes the basic elements described above. You are welcome to use or modify this for your own design:

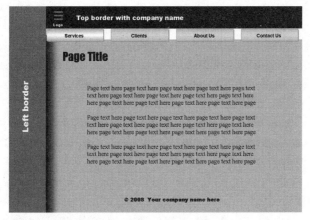

Basic standard Web page layout

Courtesy of Paula Peters and Peters Writing Services, Inc.; design done in Microsoft Publisher

Take a look at this page layout for a minute. Notice how simple it is. All the basic elements are here: top border with logo and company name, left border, navigation menu, page title, page text, and copyright statement. Notice also that they all line up as a square: left border, top border, copyright mark on the bottom. In fact, this entire layout can be designed by doing nothing more than dragging and dropping colorful squares and text boxes onto the page, which can be done in any Web or graphic design software. Pretty simple!

You can also jazz this template up, or tailor it to suit your customer preferences. Remember those customer preferences we talked about in Chapter 2, in the section "Understand Your Customer"? Now is the time to pull out that list. Is your customer earthy? Academic? Scientific? Use the preferences you noted to help guide your creation of your template. Ultimately, your customers' satisfaction is most important.

Now that you've seen a sample template, and have reviewed your customer preferences, you've probably got your own ideas floating around in your head. It's time to sketch those out. What do you want the header to look like? Do you want to include photo elements? Which direction do you want the navigation menu to run?

Whatever ideas you have, take out a blank piece of white paper, and spend five minutes drawing a simple sketch with boxes, titles, and labels, using the template above as a guideline. This will help reduce the amount of time you spend creating your page layout on the graphic design software.

For example, you might choose to include a photo in the header on your page. If you add a photo element, sketch it in your drawing and label it "photo." Show where the text will go (it's fine to just write "blah blah blah" for now—even the professionals do the same thing). Write in where your page title will go. And don't forget your logo, business name, and copyright statement.

Now is the time also to pull out your site map. See what you had planned for your navigation menu. Your menu will include all the page titles that you listed on your map. If this has changed since you created your content, update your map and include the revised version in your navigation menu.

The drawing does not have to be pretty or to scale. It just needs to give you an idea of what to place where, so that when you go to your software, you have a "map" ready to guide you. This will save you time fooling around with the software, and will shorten the process (and the frustration) immensely.

Avoid Multiple Page Layouts!

Using a consistent page layout on a small Web site makes for a better browsing experience for the user. For that reason, don't use multiple page layouts. Stick with one single page layout.

You can always create more later, when you are more experienced. It is easier, and also looks more visually pleasing for your users.

Once you have the sketch completed, you are ready to re-create it in your software or design package. Use the "Help" function (and any wizards that they offer) as much as possible. Hold off on improving the design until you get the basic one completed. Once you have done that, save it and make a copy of that file to tinker around with. Part of the fun of creating a Web site is playing around with colors and images!

Now that we've got our basic Web site page done, let's play around with it a little bit. It's easier to change only one or two design elements at a time; that way, if you don't like it, it's easier to backtrack and undo it. For example, I'd like to try adding a photo element to my page, along with a little rearranging of the spacing and sizing:

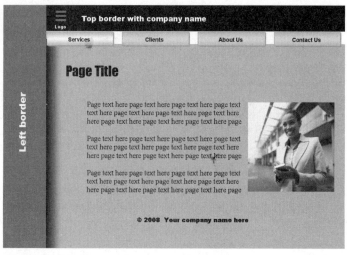

Basic standard Web page layout, with photo

Courtesy of Paula Peters and Peters Writing Services, Inc.; design done in Microsoft Publisher

Another way you can easily personalize your layout is to create a vertical navigation menu, instead of a horizontal one. Vertical navigation menus are not difficult to create, and may be more to your taste. By moving around a few squares, and playing with the top border, I come up with the following:

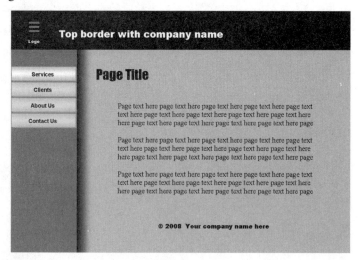

Basic standard Web page layout, with vertical navigation menu

Courtesy of Paula Peters and Peters Writing Services, Inc.; design done in Microsoft Publisher

So be creative. With a little rearranging—and a minimal investment of your time—you can come up with a unique and personalized Web page design. Or, you can stick to the simple, square layout. The choice is up to you.

Using the Right Colors in Your Design

At Peters Writing Services, we get so many questions about color that I thought I would discuss it here. Many business owners ask me, "What is the right color to use? Are there some colors that are better than others?"

The answer is: yes and no. Yes—there is an entire research field dedicated to evaluating the use of different colors in your marketing. For example, some marketing firms only use dark blue and dark green colors for clients; they have research to show that it generates more sales. That may be true. But this is a concern for a more mature business—with a lot of money to spend on marketing.

For a small business, the more important thing is to make sure that your colors in the Web site are *consistent* with the rest of your marketing materials. The colors you use in your Web site should be the same colors you use in your logo, company name, letterhead, and business cards. If you are using red and gray in your logo and on your business cards, red and gray is what you should use in your Web site. If you are using silver and blue (or pink and green, or yellow and purple), those are the same colors you should use in your Web site.

 ### Using "Dummy" Text in Your Design

You will notice in the examples I included here that I did not include "real" text—only what we call in the marketing industry "dummy" text. Sometimes we use Latin text; sometimes we say "blah blah blah" or "insert text here," or simply the word "text" over and over.

Dummy text allows you to focus on the design, instead of on the words. We process words so quickly, that it can be difficult to concentrate on colors and pictures when the words are screaming out from the page, "Spelling error! Fix it now!"

Let's go back to our original question. Is there a "right" color scheme for your Web site? Yes. It's the same color scheme that you are already using in your logo and branding.

Of course, no matter what colors you use in your branding, you will also need black. I recommend using black for the text, no matter what your branding colors are, because black is so much easier to read on a computer screen. Remember that we want to make this as easy to read as possible for your users; if it's too irritating or confusing, they'll surf elsewhere.

What If I Don't Have a Logo or Branding Color Scheme?

If you do not yet have a logo or branding color scheme designed, choose two complementary colors that work well together. Don't go crazy with too many colors; this looks amateur and can really give users a headache. If you really want a big "splash" of color, use background color or full-color photos.

 Try Using a Color Wheel

If you are not good at selecting colors, try using a color wheel. Color wheels show you very quickly which colors complement each other. They are inexpensive (usually less than $5), and can be picked up at almost any craft or art store, or you can order them at *www.dickblick.com*.

The more consistent you are with the colors in your company name and logo throughout your marketing materials, the more credible you will appear to your customers. As you are choosing your colors for the Web site, keep in mind that you'll want to replicate these colors as much as possible for your business cards, brochures, and ads in the future. Ask yourself, "Are these colors that I really like? How would they look in a marketing brochure or magazine ad?" Or, "How would they look blown up on a billboard?"

There are hundreds of great complementary color schemes you can use. You don't have to spend a lot of time, energy, or research figuring out which ones are right for you. If you spend five minutes surfing the Web, you will quickly see the color combinations that you like and dislike.

Here are a few suggestions for good complementary color schemes you can use, if you don't already have preset colors in your logo or company name:

- » Red and gray
- » Purple and green
- » Blue and silver
- » Pink and light green
- » Orange and purple
- » Forest green and navy blue
- » Black and any color

PETERS WRITING SERVICES

Peters Writing Services logo
Courtesy of Peters Writing Services, Inc.; design by Bense Garza, Garza Art & Design

Choose colors that you enjoy, that you will enjoy seeing again and again, and that you feel best represent the spirit of the business—because you will be looking at those colors *a lot* as your business grows. If you want to convey a "fun" atmosphere for your customers, choose a more fun color—like pink, purple, orange. If you have a more "serious" business, stick to more conservative colors—navy blue, silver, forest green.

Choosing the Right Font for Your Design

You may be thinking, "There are so many fonts out there. How do I choose the right one for my Web site?"

Actually, the answer is pretty simple. Although there are thousands of fonts available today, there are only a few that work well on a Web site. Many fonts are too difficult to read on a computer screen. They appear distorted by the low-resolution display format. Plus, if a font is not preloaded in the user's Web browser, he or she will not be able to read it anyway. Stick with the basic fonts when designing your Web page.

In my experience, the best choice for Web site text is black, 12-point Arial. My second choice is Times New Roman or Verdana. Even though it doesn't sound sexy, it's easy to read, safe, and is read universally by just about all Internet browsers. No matter which font you choose, you'll want to use it over and over again, on every page in your site. Be as consistent as possible throughout your design. All the text should be the same font.

Good Fonts to Use in Web Page Design

Unlike when you are designing a print brochure, where you have lots of flexibility in choosing a font, it's best to stick to the most basic fonts in when designing a Web page. This ensures that the prospective customer can actually read it.

Some common fonts for Web design:

» Arial
» Times New Roman
» Geneva
» Verdana
» Courier
» Helvetica

Check out a few of the "big" Web sites, like *www.google.com*, and you'll notice they generally follow the same guidelines.

The one exception to the rule on keeping a standard font throughout the text is your page titles. Page titles give you an opportunity to "dress up your font" a little bit. But don't go crazy here; too much color, italics, and bold makes it unreadable and amateur-looking.

A good page title is between 16- and 22-point font, and bold, black text (or one of the colors of your color scheme). It can be the same font as the rest of the text, or one of the other basic fonts. It should be positioned above the rest of the text.

Using Photographs or Pictures in Your Page Design

One easy way to personalize your Web page design is by adding photographs or pictures. This can be done simply, by adding an image to your basic page layout (as illustrated in the visual example on page 116), or by incorporating portfolio samples (see notes about the portfolio page in "Common Additional Pages").

If you decide to use photographs or pictures in your page design, there are a few special considerations to keep in mind. The first is the quality of images—from a technical standpoint as well as from an aesthetic standpoint.

Photos and pictures used on the Web site need to be in a lower resolution format, to make them easier to download for the user. For small, thumbnail images, this is usually 50 x 65 pixels; for a medium-sized product photo, it should be around 300 x 400 pixels. (A pixel is a tiny dot on your computer screen, and is used to help gauge sizes of images and pages.) A larger photo might be as large as 600 x 800 pixels. Anything larger than this may be difficult to download. If you are using a 5.1 megapixel image from a digital camera, it is producing images that are probably 2592 x 1944 pixels—and will need to be scaled down to one of the above sizes to work well on your Web site.

The good news is that because you need such low-resolution images, you can take your own pictures for the Web site—using most digital cameras. As long as the size is scaled down to one of the above sizes, you should be good to go. Even if it's taken with a fairly old or lower-quality camera, you can get probably get good enough pictures to use on your Web site. Just take the picture, download it to your computer using the camera's software, and save it. When you are ready to incorporate the image, copy and paste it where you want it in your page design. This is a real bonus for small businesses who need to have images of products in an online store.

 ## Guidelines for Web Photo Sizes

Here is a summary of the guidelines for Web photo sizes:

- » Small thumbnail photo = 50 x 65 pixels
- » Medium photo = 300 x 400 pixels
- » Large photo = 600 x 800 pixels

Remember to scale down any photos larger than this to size. If you are using a digital camera, the software that came with your camera should be able to do this. Your software may also have a feature called "Compressing" that will scale down your images to a more manageable size.

Now we get to that other tricky question—aesthetics. Just because you *can* take a photo, doesn't necessarily mean that it will look good on your Web site. In fact, a bad photo can look worse than no photo at all.

Here is what I recommend: if you are simply taking product images (or portfolio images), take your own photos. But if you want to use the photos in an artistic sense, and you are not sure of your own abilities, use stock photography.

Stock photography is a professional photo that costs much, much less because the rights are sold to many people. You can find a stock photograph of almost anything—people, places, objects, textures, and on and on. Stock photography is a great investment for a small business, because you get top-quality, professional photography, for a bargain-basement price. You can often pay less than $30 for a photo that would have cost $10,000 to create with a professional photographer to set up and take. Better yet, many stock photography Web sites now offer whole CDs of stock photography for under $400.

The best part about stock photography is that if you buy the correct ownership rights, you can reuse the photos again and again. This means that you could use the same images on your brochures, ads, and signage. It's a perfect tool for a small business with a limited budget.

So if you really want to include some good photos or images for artistic purposes, consider buying a few stock photos. They will really give your Web site a professional "sparkle." But if you are going to buy them with the intent of using them in future marketing materials, buy the rights to two versions of the photo—the high-resolution print version (for brochures, ads, and flyers), and the low-resolution version (for the Web site). Most companies offer both for a flat price.

 ## Where Can I Get Stock Photography?

There are a lot of Internet sites now where you can quickly buy stock photography. They vary greatly in price, service, and the rights available for use of the photos—so make sure you read the fine print before you buy.

» *www.istockphoto.com*
» *www.comstock.com*
» *www.gettyimages.com*
» *www.jupiterimages.com*
» *www.shutterstock.com*

Add the Content to the Layout for All Five Pages of Your Web Site

When you have finished creating your page design, you are ready to plug in the content for all five pages of your Web site. Depending on the software tool you are using, it may include a wizard to do this for you; or, you may need to actually create five (or however many) pages, then type in the text.

Whichever way it works in your software, the goal is to get all the wonderful text you wrote in the last chapter into your site design, page by page. Once you have plugged it in, you will want to make sure that each page title is correct, and is included in your navigation menu—and that all the links on the navigation menu are included on every page.

It is easier to do this with some software packages than others. In fact, some will even auto-create your navigation links with every new page you create. Then, all you need to do is go back and test the links to make sure they are working.

When you get all your pages laid out, including page titles and content, do a quick once-through to make sure that all the pages have a consistent format. Check back with your site map, and be sure that it matches. Here is a quick list of things to check for:

» Are there any missing pages?
» Are there any missing titles at the top of your pages?
» Is the navigation menu the same on every page?
» Are the colors, fonts, and lettering consistent from page to page?
» Is the header and footer in the same position on every page?
» Is the page title and body text in the same position on

every page?

It will be much easier to fix errors *before* you publish. Look closely and make any adjustments right now. If you are in doubt, ask a friend or trusted colleague to review it for you. They will likely pick up errors even more quickly than you will. Ask them to make a list, then you can step away from it for awhile and relax. When you are ready, come back . . . and fix it.

Don't Forget to Proofread!

Speaking of errors, now is the time to take care of any mistakes that might be lurking in your content. Nothing makes a Web site look more amateur than a lousy spelling error right at the top of the page. Before you publish, do a complete proofreading.

When proofreading, you are looking to correct any errors in:

- » Spelling
- » Grammar
- » Punctuation
- » Narrative voice (i.e., "I" vs. "we" or "they")
- » Facts
- » Content

Take fifteen minutes right now to go through your content line by line and fix any errors. At Peters Writing Services, we proofread all Web content before it is published; even professional writers make mistakes. My personal style as a proofreader is to read through the text three or four times, each time fixing only one thing—such as spelling, grammar, or punctuation. Many of the proofreaders I've worked with in the past, however, insist that the best way to do it is to read the text backward, and fix errors that way.

If you are really stuck and don't feel comfortable proofreading, ask a friend or colleague to help. Look for someone that enjoys reading and is good with words. Ask them to make a list of the errors. You can then go back to the Web design software and fix the errors before publishing the site. They may be able to spot things that you will miss, after spending so much time doing the writing, design, and layout.

Whichever method you use, the result will be worth it. You will have clean text, and won't have to worry about giving a bad impression to a potential new customer—all because you spelled a few words wrong.

Remember, we want to give them the best impression possible—in less than sixty seconds!

Don't Rely on Your Spellchecker!

If you are going to proofread, don't rely on the spellchecker program in your software—it rarely picks up all the errors. The best way to proofread is the long way—line by line. Luckily, most Web sites do not have too much content; for the standard five-page Web site, this should take fifteen minutes or less.

A Few Final Words . . . on Page Design

Of course, don't feel restricted by the page layout options I've suggested in this chapter. You can be as creative or experimental as you want. There are truly no right or wrong answers in Web design. Check out a few Web sites; see what you like and what you don't like. Better yet, check out your competition's Web site. You may even find some things you could do better!

Don't get discouraged that your Web site doesn't have flash, animation, video, or fancy stuff. It doesn't need to. In the end, what sells your business is your focus on the customer's benefits and needs; not whether you are using the latest technology. The prettiest Web site doesn't always sell the most deals—or products.

Besides, if a fancy Web site is really what you are after, you can still have one. If you don't have the budget, time, or technological know-how to do that, get your basic Web site up now and add the fancy stuff later. You will be in a better position then to determine whether you would enjoy trying it yourself or hiring a Web designer to make the changes for you. The important thing right now is to get your Web site up and running as quickly as possible—before you lose any more sales by not having one.

 *Chapter 6*

STEP 4: FIND A WEB HOST

B efore you can publish your Web site, you need to find a Web host. This is not a difficult step, but it's a necessary one—you don't even want to think about hosting your own Web site. (Too complicated, too much time.)

$ Total Cost: $3–$25/month (or $36–$300/year)

⏱ Total Time: 30 minutes

Considering an Online Store?

If you are even considering creating an online store at any point in the future, hire a Web host service that offers e-commerce, shopping carts, or online store functionality. It will make your life much easier later if you do create an online store, because all their tools for product listing, shipping, and credit card payment will be at your fingertips.

For more information about online stores and how they work, check out Chapter 8, under "Online Stores."

What Is a Web Hosting Service?

And, more importantly, what does it do?

The simplest explanation is this: a Web host is a company that owns a gigantic, mammoth computer that holds your Web site in its brain. A single Web hosting service can host hundreds—and sometimes thousands—of Web sites.

Whenever people type in your domain name while they are sitting at their computer, the request gets routed through several intermediate Internet service providers, then arrives at your Web host's mammoth computer. The mammoth computer displays the pages you have worked so hard to create, so the person sitting at home can see them. So, whenever a customer types in *www.peterswriting.com*, the request is routed by the Internet to my Web host, which pulls up a file with our Web site on it.

Voilà! Pure Internet magic. (Okay, maybe that's a little *too* simplistic . . . but you get the picture.)

In fact, many Web hosting services offer more than just hosting. Some offer e-mail accounts, which was critical to me in my selection of a Web host. I wanted e-mail accounts that looked like the ones you would see in a big corporation; so I got a Web host that could provide me with e-mail addresses that matched my URL, such as *paula@peterswriting.com*. You may want the same thing, so if that's important to you, find out whether or not your Web host offers that service—and how much they charge for it.

 Consider Good Service

Discount Web hosts don't always provide the best customer service (although a few are both caring and inexpensive). Consider that good service has a value, too. This is especially important during the all-important publishing process, which can be challenging for a lot of beginners. Before you choose a host, check out "Step 5: Publish the Web Site." If the publishing process seems easy to you, then you can put a priority on a low-cost provider.

Some hosting services also offer e-commerce functionality, blogs, domain name registration, design templates, and even pay-per-click marketing management. The variety of services—and prices—is amazing. Look at two or three options before making your decision. You may also want to compare a local hosting service against a national one.

Most Web hosting companies charge on a monthly basis. Annual contracts are not unusual, but you'll want to know what your commitment is before you register. Make sure you understand what you'll be paying for—and how long—before handing over your credit card number.

National vs. Local Web Hosting

There are two options for finding a Web host. You can go national, using one of the online Web hosting services; or you can go local, working with a Web hosting service in your area. Of course, there are positives and negatives to both.

For the most part, national Web host services will offer you lower prices and bigger packages with lots of options. They may also offer you speedy turnaround time. If you want cheap, fast, and quick, this is the route for you. However, be aware that many of the national services do a poor job of customer service, once you are a customer; getting help can be difficult when you need it.

In general, smaller, more local Web host service providers are competing on customer service, and you may get access directly to a Web specialist for questions and issues. Many smaller businesses—including several of my customers—are willing to pay a little more (sometimes only a few dollars more per year) for this personalized service. Some local services are also more flexible in how much service they can provide to you; they may offer month-to-month service, or may offer a low-priced maintenance fee to make regular updates to your site for you. This may be a worthwhile luxury if you plan to make regular changes to portfolios, content, samples, products, etc. Of course, if you are doing e-commerce or podcasts, for example, and feel like you just need a little extra help to get it done, going with a local Web host is definitely worth it. However, you may also want to consider that a smaller local operation may not offer the same variety of hosting features that a larger service will offer, and may not have the equipment to handle high traffic volume—or secure information transfers.

The good news is that there is no right or wrong decision. Look at a few options—both nationally and locally—and decide what's right for you. Compare prices and services, and make sure that what you are getting is the best fit for your business.

 ## Save Your Account Information!

Once you choose a Web host and set up an account with that company, save your account information. You will use this information later to publish your Web site, including the account number, user name, and password that is assigned to you.

After you publish your Web site, you will use this information to make revisions to your site (which requires you to republish), to view your site stats (such as number of visitors you receive every month), or to change your Web hosting plan.

A Few Popular Web Hosting Sites

To look for local Web hosts, check your local chamber of commerce listing or the Yellow Pages. If you are looking for national Web hosting sites, here are a few of the most popular, to get you started:

> » *www.aplus.net*
> » *www.networksolutions.com*
> » *www.1and1.com*
> » *www.bizland.com*
> » *www.verio.com*
> » *www.ipower.com*
> » *www.register.com*
> » *www.godaddy.com*
> » *www.hostmonster.com*
> » *www.startlogic.com*
> » *www.lunarpages.com*
> » *www.ixwebhosting.com*

Remember, look carefully at the fine print—know what you are getting in your package and for how long. When you are done signing up for your Web host service, you are ready to publish your Web site!

 *Chapter 7*

STEP 5: PUBLISH THE WEB SITE

$ Total Cost: $0

O kay, so you've got a domain name. Your Web site copy is well-written, and your design looks snappy. You've hired a Web hosting service that you are excited about. What's left? Publishing your Web site, of course!

🕐 Total Time: 30 minutes

Publishing is the simplest step in the process of getting your Web site up and running—but it can also be the scariest. In a few short minutes, your work will be out there on the Internet, competing with all the other sites clamoring for your customers' attention. This is an exciting step for you—and your business!

Fixing Errors Before You Publish

While it's not impossible to fix errors after you've published your Web site, it is much easier to fix them now. Take five minutes now to glance through each page, and make any final changes. Look for:

» Spelling errors
» Grammar errors
» Incorrect font (size, type, or color)
» Misplaced photos or images
» Incorrect colors
» Incorrect page titles
» Links that don't work or take you to the wrong place

So what happens when you publish your Web site? It's actually pretty simple. All you are doing is taking the files that you have written and designed, and sending them from your office to the mammoth computer at your Web host. Once there, your Web host's mammoth computer will simply display the files for anyone who requests them—meaning anyone who types your domain name into their Internet browser, anywhere in the world. See? Piece of cake.

The tricky part is getting the files to your Web host. In order to do that, you will need a few pieces of information handy:

» Your domain name (i.e. *www.mycompany.com*)
» Your Web host account user name
» Your Web host account password (probably assigned to you when you set up your Web hosting account)

There are a couple of ways you can get the files from your computer to your Web host. The procedure depends on the preferences of your Web host, and whether you designed your Web site using software—or using an online design service package.

Publishing Your Site Using an Online Design Service Package

If you designed your Web site using an online service that provided templates and hosting, your files are probably already stored on the service's computers. All you need to do is activate their publishing process and you are done.

You will need step-by-step instructions from your online Web design service. The best place to start is at your account page. Access the files you have created, and look for a publishing option or button. Most Web hosts now offer direct publishing using a link on their site (usually located on your account's page, once you log in). They also have step-by-step instructions for getting your files published onto the Internet.

Publishing Your Site Using a Computer-Based Software

If you have created your Web site using a software on your own computer, you need to get the files transferred from your computer to your Web host. There are a couple of ways to do this:

» Through a "Publish" function or wizard in your software
» Through a designated link on your Web hosting site
» Through an FTP site

If your software offers a "Publish" function, or wizard, use it—it will be the simplest way to get the files transferred. It will walk you through the steps, one at a time, for transferring the files to your Web host. It will also establish your files and preferences for later usage, in case you decide to edit or change content and designs at a future date. Using the software's "Publish" function will also allow you to access their Help functionality.

If your software does not offer a "Publish" function or if you find it too confusing to use, check out your Web hosting site. If you log into your account, you should be able to find step-by-step instructions for uploading your Web site files and getting it running "live." Of course, your Web host is highly motivated to get you up and running with your Web site, so they can earn your money—so if you have any difficulties, you can also get the benefit of using their customer support, whether it's a call-in phone support or live chat support service via the Internet.

Finally, be aware that some Web hosts require you to submit your files through what is called an FTP site (sounds intimidating, but actually is quite simple). An FTP (file transfer protocol) site includes a special link that is geared to accept and upload large files very quickly. If your Web host uses this process, they should give you a Web address, login name, and password to access the FTP site.

What If I Don't See My Web Site Immediately?

No matter which way you publish—or which way you created your original files, software or online service—you should see your published Web site files within a few minutes (but no later than twenty minutes). You may even see them immediately.

If you do not see your Web site display on an Internet browser within twenty minutes after you've published it, something is wrong. This is not uncommon—experienced Web designers find that the systems can be so finicky, even *they* have to try a few times.

If you don't see your Web site displayed when you type in your domain name, click the "Refresh" button on your Internet browser. This will remove any older stuff from your computer's memory, and will make sure you are viewing the "latest and greatest" information. Some people like to go to another computer and see it—just to be sure it's working correctly on a different computer.

If that trick doesn't display the Web site, and you've waited several minutes for it to publish, the easiest thing to do is try publishing it again. Go through the same steps, and the same process. Make sure all file names are typed exactly correct—even a single missed period can mean the difference between success and failure.

Try republishing it a couple of times. If you still are not having success, and you've waited a few minutes to see it, contact your Web host's customer service.

Adding Keywords and a One-Sentence Description

One of your final steps when you publish your Web site is to add keywords and a short, one-sentence description to it. These words allow the search engines to pick up your Web site and list your services and products. Ideally, your business name, product, or service should be easy for your customers to find when they do a search. But be warned: search engine optimization has become a tricky and sophisticated game (see Chapter 9 for more details).

You can do this in the control panel of your Web hosting account. Usually, each page has a function called "Properties," which lists a metadescription, metakeywords, and/or metatags. Your metadescription—or one-sentence description of your business—should be short, and describe your business simply (in twenty-five words or less). The keywords should be single words or phrases, and include (at a minimum) the name of your business, and your key products or services.

Check your Web host FAQs to see if there is a limit to how many keywords you include per page. For example, we typically include between twenty and fifty keywords on our Web site, *www.peterswriting.com*. My keyword list includes the following words and phrases (among others):

> » Paula Peters
> » Peters Writing Services
> » Technical writing
> » Procedure manuals
> » Curriculum design
> » Marketing materials
> » Government RFP

Make sure your keywords and description accurately describe your products, services, and business name.

Don't Even Think About Lying!

Don't even think about lying in your description or keywords. Search engines will pick up on this and blacklist you. And that's the last thing you want to have happen to your brand-new Web site!

Testing the Web Site Functionality

Once your Web site is up and running, do a little testing. Click through the menus, links, and navigation. Does everything look right? Are all the links working correctly? Did all the information get uploaded correctly?

If anything is broken, missing, or not working correctly, now is the time to fix it. Don't wait for a customer to find an error for you! (There is no more embarrassing conversation to have than "Did you know that your Web site isn't working?" Trust me.) And if there is really a major issue, you can always fix it in your personal Web site files on your computer (or in your online account), and then republish it.

What If I Need to Fix Something . . . *After* I've Published My Site?

To correct an error on your Web site—whether it's content, design, or navigation functionality—you will not actually fix it on the "live" Web site. Go back to your original Web site files (on your computer or in your account with the online design package service, depending on where you originally created them). Fix the error, then resave the files. When you are finished, go through the publishing process again—only this time, publish the newly corrected files that you just saved.

When you are done, and everything is in working order, it's time for a little celebration. Congratulations! You are now the proud parent of a brand new Web site.

 *Chapter 8*

ADD OTHER FUNCTIONS TO YOUR WEB SITE

Feeling adventurous? Ready to try a blog? Want to set up an online store? Then read on for information on some of the most intriguing new functions for Web sites—and how they can help your business. You will be surprised by how much is now available in an affordable (and easy-to-use) format, even for a beginner. Good luck!

Blogs

You may have heard about blogs, but don't know what they are—or what all the buzz is about. Or maybe you'd like to try one, but are afraid it's too much to tackle for your first Web site. A blog may or may not be right for your business—it depends on your interest level, time availability, and your customer audience. But whatever your personal feelings about blogs, when they are used correctly, they can really help a new business looking to build relationships with customers.

What Is a Blog?

In its simplest form, a blog is nothing more than an online diary, where someone (the "blogger") posts comments on his or her Web site on a regular basis. Blogs typically include ideas, insights, opinions, suggestions, and ramblings about anything—and everything—important to the blogger. These comments are very individualized and personalized.

Usually, a blog allows comments, questions, and feedback from readers (or customers). But not always. Sometimes, a blog is limited only to the comments and ideas of the Web site owner.

Why Do I Want a Blog?

There are a few reasons why a blog might be a good choice for your business. If you really have something to say and you want to have a voice in your community, it's a good tool for sharing opinions and ideas with your current—and potential—customers. Blogs can also help you get listed higher up in search engines, especially if you are discussing specific terms that are easily searchable on engines like Google, MSN, or Yahoo!.

A blog is also a nice way to show potential customers a different side to you. While your regular Web site gives them all the "nuts and bolts" information, a blog shows your "softer side" by sharing your opinions and ideas. It can help solidify their image of you as an expert in your field if you give sound, practical advice in your area of expertise. This works especially well for artists, landscapers, and designers.

Blog Sites

If you are really more interested in creating a blog than a Web site, try using a blog site service. This is a site that is just dedicated to blogging—and not much else. These sites either sell blog space or offer it for free on a larger, master site where you can create your own blog page, but not necessarily create an entire Web site. You will likely be one of many hundreds of people on the same virtual space, each logging your own blog pages. But beware—advertising supported blog spaces may actually feature ads for your competitors right alongside your content!

If you are interested in just creating a blog for your customers, rather than listing your services, products, clients, and company information, why not skip the Web site, and just create the blog? Here are a few sites to check out:

> » *www.blogger.com*
> » *www.myspace.com*
> » *www.mytypes.com*
> » *www.squarespace.com*

You should be aware that if you don't have time to update your blog regularly, it may be a waste of your time. A "dead blog" that hasn't been updated in weeks or months looks bad to a potential customer—like you are out of business, or just not current. The best blogs are updated daily; but weekly—or even monthly—is okay, too, as long as there is a regular history of comments, preferably on a wide variety of topics related to your business. If you can't regularly make time to update your blog, it may not be the right choice for you.

How Do I Create a Blog?

There are four ways to create a blog:

1. Create a page on a blog site.
2. Use the blog function in your Web design software (if available).
3. Use the blog service provided by your Web host (if available).
4. Get a blog plug-in to fit with your Web site.

Create a Page on a Blog Site

By far, the easiest way to do it is to go to an existing blog site and create a page with your blog. While it may cost you some money, many services are now doing it for free. The blog site will host your blog, help you manage the comments and replies, and even offer some measure of security and confidentiality. All you need to do is set up an account, create your page using one of their template designs, and personalize it as much as you want with colors, photos, etc. Then you are ready to start sharing your opinions to the world. The blog site retains the control (and domain name) of your blog page.

While this is the fastest and easiest way to set up—and maintain—a blog, there are also some disadvantages. For example, it will not be connected to your Web site, domain name, URL, or business name—you are "renting" space on a larger Web site (such as *www.myspace.com*). If making your blog a part of your Web site is important to you, or if you want to make sure your business name and branding are front and center, create a blog on your own Web site.

Not only that, but some of the free, advertising-supported blog sites may post ads related to the blogging topic. This is normal; it's how they earn a living. However, it may mean that if you are discussing a business topic, your competitors' ads may be featured right alongside your blog!

Use the Blog Function in Your Web Design Software (If Available)

Some versions of Web design software now offer a blog option. The software actually allows you to create a blog page, author your comments, and then publish them as part of your Web site. For example, Adobe Contribute allows multiple users to blog and publish on the same Web page, using their standard Web design functionality.

If you have already bought your Web design software, check out the packaging or the help file. See if blogging capability exists. This may be your easiest—and simplest—way to go if you want to retain control over your Web site and branding, but still publish a blog as easily as possible. Use the wizard, or step-by-step instructions included in your software's help file, to show you how to create and publish it.

Use the Blog Service Provided by Your Web Host (If Available)

If your Web host offers blog functionality, use it. Many Web hosts are now offering a blog setup and maintenance program for a very small monthly fee (and for some, it's a free additional service).

If you've already selected a Web host, check out their options for hosting a blog—including the cost and what it will look like when finished. You'll want to find out: Will it be a part of your Web site, or will it take the customer to another site altogether?

Web Hosts That Offer Blog Services

There are now several Web hosting services that offer blogs for their Web host customers. If your Web host already offers a blog service, you are in luck. Be sure to check out the fine print, and understand how it works, what it will look like, and how much it will cost.

A few Web hosts that are now offering blog capability to their customers:

» *www.godaddy.com*
» *www.aplus.net*
» *www.verio.com*
» *www.squarespace.com*
» *www.hostmonster.com*

If the Web host option works for you, go for it. This will be the easiest way for you to get your blog published, even easier than creating it yourself with your own Web design software.

Get a Blog Plug-In to Fit with Your Web Site

If you don't have a Web design software (or a Web host provider) that comes with blog functionality, but you'd prefer not to use a blog host site, get a blog plug-in that will fit with your Web site. A plug-in is an additional software that you can install. It uses a template to create a blog page that's part of your own Web site, and allows you to manage it yourself.

But be aware—there aren't many companies that offer this service. And they may not be easy for a beginner to use. So investigate your plug-in carefully before you buy. In the end, you may decide it's easier to switch to a Web host that offers blog capability—or that you'd rather buy a Web design software that does the same.

 Where Can I Get a Blog Plug-In?

There are only a few companies that offer blogs that plug in to your existing Web site. Study them carefully before you purchase, and make sure that they will work with your Web host and/or Web design software. Also, make sure that the one you choose will be easy enough to manage on your own. Start by checking out *www.typepad.com*.

How Does a Blog Work?

A blog is simple to create, whether you are working from a software, a Web host, or a stand-alone blog service. Basically, all you need to do is:

1.   Set up an account with the Web host or blog service (doesn't apply if you are using your own Web design software).
2.   Choose the page layout template for your blog page.
3.   Customize the design with your own images.
4.   Set the management options for your blog (for user comments, etc.).
5.   Write your first entry.
6.   Publish your blog.

While the actual steps may vary from service to service, or from software to software, this overview gives you the basics. Once you register with your blog or Web host service, or purchase your Web design software, you can check out their step-by-step instructions on how to execute the specific steps, including writing, customizing, and publishing your own blog.

Once you start writing your entries, you will want to write regularly—daily, weekly, or at a minimum, monthly. Write about any topic that you think might interest your customers. Some good ideas for blog topics include:

- » New product info
- » Do-it-yourself tips
- » Industry information
- » New trends
- » Ideas for reducing costs
- » Ideas for improving quality of life

Check Out a Few Blogs First

Before you begin writing your own blog, spend some time looking at a few blog sites. Notice the things you like and don't like. Which topics work really well? Which don't? What seems to be the right length for a discussion?

After reading a few, you'll get a good idea of what you like, and what you don't. For starters, you can try browsing through *www.blogger.com*, which often features links to interesting blogs on its home page. But be warned— blogging is fun, and can be addictive!

Your blog entries don't have to be long. Even a fifty- or 100-word entry should cover any topic, within reason. The more frequently you blog, the shorter your entries can be; I would not recommend an entry longer than 500 words. Anything longer, and you risk losing your reader. People just do not have the time or attention span to read such a long essay on the Web.

Keys to Success with Blogs

If you are going to use a blog to help promote your business or your Web site, there are a few things that you'll want to do to make sure it is successful.

Regular Updates

I'll say it again: A blog must be updated regularly to be successful. An unused, outdated blog looks worse than having no blog at all. If you cannot update it with new entries at least monthly (better yet—weekly, or even daily), don't spend the time to create one. You're time (and money) will be better spent elsewhere in your business.

Customer-Focused Topics

To make a blog really interesting for customers, you need to write about topics that are interesting to them. While the latest antics of your cat may be funny, they may not entice readers to buy products from you.

Listen to the questions customers ask you. Find out what they are interested in. Write short, sweet segments about these topics, and you'll come out a winner.

Podcasts

Next to blogs, podcasts are the hottest thing in Web site design today. But are they right for your Web site? If you are considering adding a podcast to your site, read on for more details about the pros—and cons.

What Is a Podcast?

A podcast may sound high-tech, but really, it's nothing more than a short audio broadcast—kind of like a mini-radio broadcast. The only difference is that it's usually produced by amateurs and distributed on the Internet, not on a radio.

In a typical podcast, a person records himself talking or interviewing other people. A computer microphone records the broadcast, then specialized software picks up the recording and converts it into an electronic file (usually an MP3 file). The podcast is then put on a Web site for other people to find and download, and the file can be listened to on an iPod, an MP3 player, or other software (like the iTunes Player).

 Want to Hear an Example of a Podcast?

Curious about podcasts, and want to know what they sound like? Check out the podcasts offered on one of the many new Web sites that offer podcast posting, much like blog posting:

» *www.podHoster.com*
» *www.podcastalley.com*

Note—before you listen to your first podcast, download a software to your computer that allows you to play podcasts. (If you have an iPod or MP3 player, you probably already have the software.) Most podcast Web sites offer a list of downloadable player software, but you can get the popular iTunes player free from Apple at *www.apple.com/itunes*.

Most podcasts are short, usually between one and three minutes, although some are longer. They can include interviews, seminars, instruction manuals, or book readings. In the business world, they tend to focus on a "hot topic"—a trend, an idea, or an opinion.

Why Do I Want a Podcast?

A podcast gives you an opportunity to connect to new customers, or to stay connected to your current customers, by communicating to them about some aspect of their life or industry. A podcast is a fun, interactive way to express your ideas and opinions to your customers.

While it does require a time commitment to set up and create your first one, successive podcasts will be easier to do, and they can often be tagged onto blogs. Your customers (or prospective customers) can download your commentary, and listen to it on their computer, MP3 player, or iPod.

How Do I Create a Podcast?

Here are the basic steps for creating a podcast:

1. Purchase and install the necessary computer equipment. At a minimum, you'll need a computer microphone and podcasting software (either a standalone podcasting software, or through a Web site).
2. Record your podcast.
3. Test your podcast by listening to it. Rerecord (or edit out) any portions that you are not happy with.
4. Publish your podcast onto a Web site (either your own, or a site dedicated to podcasts).

The easiest option for beginners is to use a dedicated podcast Web site. These sites provide all the software and hosting options for a minimal monthly fee; you may even be able to link the URL of the podcast site to your own Web site. All you have to do is create an account, download the software, set up your microphone, and start podcasting.

 Quick and Easy Podcast Web Sites

A variety of Web sites now offer podcast creation, production, publication, and hosting—often for a small setup and monthly fee. Checkout a few of the most popular:

- » *www.podHoster.com*
- » *www.podcastpeople.com*
- » *www.mypodcast.com*
- » *www.podcastalley.com*

You can even find topic-specific podcast sites. For example, if you are a religious organization, such as a church or Bible group, you'll find *www. altarcast.com* interesting. They are dedicated strictly to hosting podcasts from religious organizations, including sermons and lessons. You might want to see if there is a specific site that caters to your customer audience market.

Try your own Web host, too. Several Web host providers are now offering a podcast hosting option, which may (or may not) be able to link directly to your own individualized Web site. For example, *www.godaddy .com* offers a service to their Web hosting customers called Quick Podcast, allowing you to quickly—and easily—add a podcast to your Web site. Check out your own Web host to see if they provide a podcast service option before you try a dedicated podcast Web site, and make sure you understand what the cost is before you sign up.

Keys to Success with Podcasts

If you decide to offer podcasts on your Web site, consider a few keys to success.

Pertinent Topics

If you are using your podcasts to build a rapport with your listening audience, and ultimately to entice them to buy from you, consider your topics very carefully. Descriptions of your family vacation are not going to fly with busy customers who can barely squeeze sixty seconds out of their day for your podcast.

Make your podcast short, to the point, and focused on a topic that is interesting to your *customer*, not to you. A few good topics:

> » Ideas for saving money
> » Ideas for saving time
> » Discussion of trends in the industry
> » New products that customers might like
> » Step-by-step how-to instructions
> » Customer testimonials about your products or services
> » Interviews of key experts in your field

Just like with any good marketing materials—whether that's a brochure, a Web site, or a press release—a good podcast will be much more effective in attracting customers to your business if it focuses on the *customer's* wants and needs.

Good Recording Equipment

Just like in a real radio broadcast studio, the better the equipment, the better the podcast. If you are only experimenting with podcasts for fun, and not really interested in doing them long-term, don't bother spending a lot of money on the equipment. However, if the podcasts are a key part of your marketing strategy, take the time to purchase the right equipment for your computer—including the right software, microphone, and speaker equipment. While it may cost you more money upfront, in the long run, you'll be glad you did it. Make sure that the audio quality is good, and that it is compatible with the computer equipment where it will be used.

Online Stores

Believe it or not, new entrepreneurs create online stores all the time—even those with very little Web design or graphic experience. They are out there selling products for their own small businesses right now. And you can, too.

If you are looking to sell products online, don't be intimidated by the prospect of creating an online store. With a little bit of time and money, you can have your own online store up and running in no time.

What Is an Online Store?

An online store is exactly what it sounds like—a Web site location where you can sell your products and services. It can be used to sell three products or 300. In fact, it's a complete virtual retail facility that conducts the entire sales transaction for you, just like a regular storefront—but without the expensive brick-and-mortar overhead costs. It handles your:

» Product displays
» Checkout process
» Credit card payments
» Shipping

It Doesn't Have to Be One or the Other

Even if you already have a brick-and-mortar store, you can still benefit from an online store. Your online store can add powerful upselling and cross-selling capability to an established base of customers. And you can reach a broader base of customers—including those who don't live in your area.

For more tips about maximizing your new online store (with or without an existing storefront business), see Chapter 9.

Why Do I Want an Online Store?

Online stores are incredibly powerful. They can provide a broader range of products than many entrepreneurs can afford to carry in a storefront. You can reach more people—not just in your town, but across the globe, especially if you carry a niche product. And best of all, it costs much less to operate an online store than a traditional brick-and-mortar store. In this case, your investment is not in a lease, utilities, signage, and window dressing, but rather in technology, secure processing, and marketing.

In my mind, however, the real advantage of your online store is that it is a low-commitment venture. You can get it up and running very quickly—

and add products as you go. You don't have to sign your life away for a five-year lease and insurance; you can have it up and running in a couple of days with a few products, and then keep adding to it so that it grows organically. It is ideal for the business owner who wants to start out small and grow the store as the business makes more money.

How Do I Create an Online Store?

Let's be honest here—you don't have hours and hours to create an online store from scratch. Nor would you want to, even if you could (too many security risks). The easiest way to create an online store is to buy or rent one, and then just plug in your items for sale. While some Web design software packages now offer a shopping cart or an e-commerce function, you will save yourself a lot of time, headache, and hassle by just working with a prepackaged one.

There are a few ways you can do this:

1. Hire a Web host that offers online stores.
2. Use a third-party e-commerce service.
3. Sell your products through a larger online marketplace.

Hire a Web Host That Offers Online Stores

The easiest way to get an online store up and running is to hire a Web host that offers online stores. These services will not only publish and host your Web site once it's done, but for a small additional fee, they will also handle all the processing for your online store. All you do is add your product photos, descriptions, pricing, and shipping information.

 Web Hosts that Offer Online Store Functions

If there is even the slightest chance that you might want to someday open your own online store, you will save yourself a lot of time and trouble later by hiring a Web host that already has instant online store functionality (also called shopping cart or e-commerce). The following popular hosting sites offer online store hosting packages:

» *www.aplus.net*

> » *www.godaddy.com*
> » *www.networksolutions.com*
> » *www.verio.com*
> » *www.register.com*

The good news is that as competition for online store service has increased, the price for the business owner has gone down. Many Web hosts are now handling your online store processing for a startup fee when you register your account, and then a small monthly fee—with no long-term commitments. For a new business owner with little cash, you can't beat it!

Best of all, most of them already include all the tools you need for running your online store, including:

> » Virtual cataloging tools for your products—you just add description, photo, and pricing
> » Credit card processing
> » Shipping tables
> » Order tracking
> » Fraud protection

Even if you don't necessarily need the shopping functionality now, it will make your life a lot easier if you *do* decide to set up a store at a future date; you won't have to switch Web hosts, for example, which can be a hassle.

What If I Already Hired a Web Host, but Now I Want to an Online Store?

If you have already hired a Web host, but have now decided that you'd like to do an online store, don't panic. It's possible that your Web hosting service already provides this option, but that you just hadn't registered for it.

Spend a few minutes investigating whether or not your Web host offers e-commerce, shopping cart, or online store functionality. Check out their Web site, e-mail their customer service, or call their help line. Even if they don't offer this service, there's still no reason to panic—you can always use a third-party e-commerce service, or sell your products through a larger online marketplace, like Amazon. com or eBay. If worse comes to worst, you can always change Web hosts.

Use a Third-Party E-Commerce Service

You can also use a third party e-commerce service, instead of using a Web host, to provide online store functionality for you. A third party e-commerce service lists and sells your products on their own site. (Some do offer the functionality to "appear" as though it is selling through your site, but not all.) While it will directly be a part of your own Web site, it also takes care of a lot of details, such as payment processing, hosting, etc. The goal is to save you time, and make the processing easier for you. Some can also start the transaction at your site, then take the customer to their site to finalize the transaction.

One of the major advantages of offering this service—instead of offering items for sale directly on your Web site—is that many customers trust the third party providers more with their credit card information. While you lose the branding and personalization of conducting the entire transaction yourself, you also gain a large measure of security and confidence from the prospective customer.

To make sure that this option is right for you, take a few minutes to check out the services available before you purchase. Services in this market are changing every day, and new offerings are being developed yearly. Prices are also coming down significantly.

Third Party E-Commerce Services

A few of the more popular third party e-commerce services include:

» *http://googlecheckout.com*
» *http://smallbusiness.yahoo.com/ecommerce/*
» *www.paypal.com*

Sell Your Products Through a Larger Online Marketplace

Have you considered selling your products through a larger online marketplace, such as eBay or Amazon?

Even if you are already committed to creating your own online store, don't discount the impact that these large online clearinghouses may have on your sales. Many Web experts have told me that businesses with established online stores still get a good percentage of their sales through eBay and Amazon.

If you are thinking, "No way, eBay is an auction site for hobbyists," think again. EBay has actually become a very large reseller of new products, with a large niche following. It allows you to create your own store and list products in a standard online store format—using photography, descriptions, shipping policies, etc. Amazon.com does the same thing. And while you don't build the one-on-one relationship with the customer that you might with your own virtual storefront, it can still bring you some great sales.

 Large Online Marketplaces

eBay isn't just for hobbyists anymore. Serious merchants are selling their high-quality products using online stores at such places as:

- » *www.ebay.com*
- » *www.amazon.com*
- » *www.shopping.com*
- » *www.sell.com*

How Does an Online Store Work?

In order to create your online store, you will first need to select your online store provider—whether that's a Web host, a third party provider, or a large marketplace. After that, there are only a few basic steps to follow. Your provider will offer the specific, step-by-step instructions for ramping up your store. However, here is an overview of the process:

Step #1: Choose your online store/e-commerce service provider.

Step #2: Set up an account.

Step #3: Add your product information—including photos, descriptions, pricing, payment processing, and shipping info.

Step #4: Publish your storefront.

Step #5: Begin selling!

Remember, you can always get a few products up and running to start, see how you like it, then add more later. It's no problem to build a little bit at a time. Don't be shy about starting with just a single item!

Running a Nonprofit Organization Online?

Even if you are running a nonprofit organization online and would like to sell items or take donations, you can find a service provider that is geared toward nonprofits. Check out www.convio.com, which has a store-building service, or www.paypal.com, which can set up nonprofit Web sites with a button that says "Donate Now."

Keys to Success with Online Stores

Online stores, unlike a plain old Web site, require some additional care and maintenance to be successful. If you are going to make it work well, there are a few keys to success to consider.

Security

If customers don't feel comfortable handing over their credit card numbers to you, they won't buy from you. Period. You must make sure that your online store is as secure as possible.

What does this mean? This means that you will make every effort possible to protect the confidential information of your customers—not just their credit card information, but their names and addresses.

And it's not just for the benefit of your customers. If your site gets hacked by a criminal, and credit card numbers and personal information are stolen, *you* will be responsible—just like in a traditional storefront break-in. This is not a situation that a new entrepreneur wants during their first year in business (or any time, for that matter)!

Take as many security precautions as you can afford. For example, make sure that your online store provider (or third-party payment processor) uses SSL (secure sockets layer) encryption for the data. Some people won't buy anything from a Web site unless it shows the "lock" icon. And post your security policy on your Web site for your customers to see.

If you really want to be safe, and you only have a few products to sell, stick with selling through a larger online marketplace, like Amazon.com or eBay. They will handle any customer data or financial security issues for you (although you will still be responsible for order fulfillment and customer service).

 ## E-Commerce Software

If you are the kind of person who enjoys tinkering on your computer, you may enjoy purchasing an actual e-commerce software and starting from scratch. It will allow you greater control over creating the online store experience. A few to try:

» *www.storebuilder.com*
» *www.storefront.net*
» *www.jstreettech.com*
» *www.ecommercetemplates.com* (offers online store templates that are fully integratable with such Web design software as Dreamweaver and Frontpage)

Just be aware that your time investment will increase with the use of your own software.

Marketing

If you are going to be selling your products exclusively through an online store, with no traditional brick-and-mortar storefront, you will need to rely heavily on Internet marketing of your store (see Chapter 9). Some of my clients tell me that online stores get as much as 50 percent of their total sales through pay-per-click marketing.

If you are selling exclusively through the Internet and do not have a customer base to interface and market to immediately, plan on investing time, money, and energy into pay-per-click marketing.

Customer Service

Your customer service policies—including your availability to answer questions, your shipping policy, and your return policy—are as important to the sale as your online storefront. Spend some time thinking through your policies, and how you'd like to handle each of these customer service issues *before* you publish your store. Then post your policies on your site. A quick page with a bullet list of policies, or even a FAQs page, should do the trick. Let customers know that you are going to treat them well, and that they can reach a "live person" if they need to. (You don't need to be there twenty-four hours a day, but you need to at least be available if there is a question during the purchasing process—or available to call back as quickly as possible.)

Above all, don't be intimidated by the process of creating an online store. Even if you have absolutely no experience with Web or graphic design whatsoever, you can do it. The tools available today are easy enough—and inexpensive enough—to experiment, and come up with a great store . . . all by yourself!

Chapter 9

MARKET YOUR BUSINESS WITH YOUR NEW WEB SITE

Now that you have created your new Web site, you are ready to make it work for you—by marketing your business. Remember, a good Web site is a living, evolving entity. If you want your Web site to help your business, you need to really maximize its visibility. Very few people will happen upon your Web site "by accident." Like any landmark, they need to know that it's out there first, so they know to visit it.

Don't Neglect Your Web Site!

One of the biggest mistakes new business owners make is to create a beautiful Web site, then allow it to sit, untouched, for years. If you truly want to maximize your return on the time and money you spent on your Web site, treat it as a tool to market your business. And just like any other marketing tool (such as a brochure, press release, or Yellow Pages ad), it will require a little creativity—and experimentation—to get it right.

Setting Goals for Your Web Marketing

The good news is that all types of businesses market themselves on the Internet. You will find businesses with only one person, and businesses with 100,000 people; you will see product businesses and service businesses; as well as brand-new businesses, and businesses that are fifty years old (and older). No matter where you are in the life cycle of your business, your Web site can help you market your business.

As you mull over the possibilities of how you can use that site to market your business, consider your goals. Go back to the goals you created in Chapter 2, in the section, "Set Reasonable Goals for Your Web Site." Did you include any goals about marketing? If not, perhaps it's time to add some. What do you want to accomplish by marketing your Web site? How would you like the Internet to help your business? You will be sure to achieve more of what you want by clarifying those goals.

The most common goals for marketing a Web site are:

» Bring in new leads for prospective customers
» Sell more products or services
» Increase repeat business among current customers

> » Act as a "credibility tool" for your business, to help create customer confidence (and close deals)

Be creative. Set up your own goals. Then, with a little elbow grease and some experimentation, you can try different things to see what works for *your* business. In a few months, schedule time to revisit your goals, measure your progress ... and see if they still make sense for you.

How Your New Web Site Will Benefit Your Business

Whether you sell products or services, your new web site can help your business by bringing you new leads and customers. It can also be used to demonstrate to prospective customers that you are a legitimate business.

Yes, Service Businesses *Can* Benefit from a Web Site

Many service business owners tell me, "A Web site is a waste of time for my business. We don't sell widgets. We sell consulting services/staffing services/facilities maintenance/landscaping services." But they are wrong. It's an absolute myth that Web sites cannot benefit service business. In fact, the Internet can give a service-based business a distinct advantage over competitors, and can even help an established business bring in the extra leads and revenue that it needs. Many, many service-based businesses use their Web sites to sell—including mine, Peters Writing Services.

Here are the three main ways that your new Web site will benefit your business:

1. Serving as a "credibility tool" to help close deals
2. Bringing in new leads through Internet marketing
3. Selling directly to new and current customers

Use #1: Serve as a "Credibility Tool" to Help Close Deals

The best—and easiest—use of the Web site for a business is as a credibility tool to help close deals. Using your Web site as a credibility tool requires very little energy or effort on your part. All you need to do is to share your Web site with your prospective customers when you talk with them—on the phone, in your store, through an e-mail, or in a sales meeting. That's it. That's all. Just give them your Web address and suggest that they visit it to learn more about you. It can be as casual as saying, "Thank you for taking the time to talk with me today. If you are interested in our work, you might like to see more about us at *www.xyzcompany.com*."

Once your phone call or meeting is over, an interested prospective customer will naturally visit your Web site. (Trust me—if they are interested in doing business with you, they'll check you out.) Once your potential customer visits your Web site, he or she can see how professional it is. And suddenly, they say to themselves, "Wow . . . this guy is for real." This makes the sales process quicker, simpler, and easier. And this is how a majority of small businesses utilize their Web site.

 ## Get the Whole Team Involved!

If you are the only employee, then it's easy to mention your Web site in every conversation with a customer. If, however, you have two or more people working on your team, make sure everyone is mentioning your Web site on a regular basis—through phone calls, e-mails, and sales conversations. Discuss this with them first, then follow up routinely to ensure that they are notifying customers of your Web site address. After all—if nobody knows about it, nobody will see it!

Of course, this education process isn't limited to a verbal conversation with your customer. For maximum effectiveness, you'll want to make sure that you mention your Web site address in every piece of marketing literature that reaches a new, prospective customer during the sales process. (And this includes anyone who could *become* a prospective customer at a future date—such as association members, colleagues, and neighbors.) Don't forget to add your Web site address to your:

» Business cards
» Letterhead
» E-mails
» Brochures
» Trade show booths
» Newspaper ads
» Yellow Pages ads
» Invoices
» Sales quotes or estimates

The goal is for any prospective customer to see your Web site, and say, "Hey! This is a genuine business. They have a nice Web site. They are professionals; they are *not* hucksters." That's why we call it a credibility tool.

The reason that this is so important is that customers won't buy from businesses they don't trust. Customers constantly look for visual and verbal cues that a business is legitimate. Without that confidence, there is simply no sale—especially from a service business, where there is no "product" and very often, the service is intangible. A Web site can inspire that consumer confidence in your business, much like the business card—or storefront—of yesteryear. It shows that you are *real*.

So try it. As soon as your Web site is up and running—that very same day—begin talking it up with your customers, new contacts, and colleagues. Mention it in every sales meeting, on every customer phone call, in every e-mail. This takes very little energy or effort. You now have a powerful tool that can mean the difference between a deal—and no deal.

 ### The Value of a Portfolio for a Service Business

If you are a service business that lacks a tangible product, a portfolio on your Web site can add a little bit of extra credibility. It's like displaying a catalog of completed projects. With that visual reference, customers feel more confident buying from you. Check out the section on the "Samples or Portfolios Page." It's easy, and will be worth the little extra effort to create if it helps you sell another two or three deals this year.

Use #2: Bring in New Leads Through Internet Marketing

Once you are regularly educating your prospective customers about your Web site during your sales process, it's time to think about bringing in entirely new leads through your Web site. What do I mean by "new leads"? These are prospective customers that have never done business with you, and in fact, don't even know you exist. They find you entirely through your Web site.

Sound impossible? It's not! It's the magic of the Internet. Talking it up with your prospective (and current) customers is one way to spread the word about your site. However, if you really want to drive traffic to your Web site—especially traffic from customers you've never met or who are spread out across the world—invest a little bit of time and money into understanding the Internet game.

There are a few different strategies to get new leads to your Web site, which we will discuss in more detail later. These are: search engine optimization, pay-per-click advertising, selling through large online marketplaces, and blogs.

Use #3: Sell Directly to New and Current Customers

Of course, the third—and final—major use of your new Web site is to sell directly to new and current customers. For product businesses, this can be done with e-commerce, or by selling through large online marketplaces. But even service businesses can sell directly through the Internet, so don't assume that you cannot sell your services online just because you are a service business.

In order to sell over the Internet, of course, you will need to turn your Internet site into a sort of online catalog, with accurate descriptions of your services, and a shopping cart function.

However, if you are willing to take a few risks, and you have the kind of business that can support a Web-based sales model, consider selling your services right over the Internet. With a little bit of experimentation, you can make a wide variety of service businesses work with Internet sales.

The Top Four Internet Marketing Techniques for Small Business

Okay, so you are using your new Web site as a credibility tool, and customers are starting to take notice. Where do you go from there?

If you are looking to attract more visitors to your Web site, then you may want to consider trying one of these top four Internet marketing techniques, which work perfectly for smaller businesses and organizations.

1. Keyword optimization for search engines
2. Pay-per-click advertising
3. Large online marketplaces
4. Blogs

Keyword Optimization for Search Engines

Keyword optimization for search engines is a technique for getting your Web site included in the results of a Web search. When a person searches for a particular word on a search engine like Google, Yahoo!, or MSN, those search engines utilize the keywords and metatags that you provide in the properties of your Web site. For example, if a person is searching for antique lanterns, and they find an antique lantern dealer offering 759 varieties of antique lanterns at the top of the list, it is very likely that the dealer is using search engine optimization to ensure that he or she is at the top of the list.

One way that you can get your products included in the search engines is to optimize the keywords on your Web site. This method of marketing has gained a lot of media attention in recent years, and has become quite an Internet phenomenon. The goal is to finagle your Web site's keywords in such a way that your Web site gets "bumped up" as close as possible to the top of the list whenever someone performs a search for that keyword on a major search engine (such as Google). While it's not always possible—or feasible—to be bumped up to the top of the list for a particular keyword, you should at least do the minimum effort required to ensure that your Web site is being included in a standard Internet search.

For example, if you sell gift baskets with prepackaged sticky buns, you will definitely want to add the keywords "sticky buns" to your site—as well as "cinnamon rolls," "sweet rolls," "gift baskets," and "gift packages." The goal is for anyone searching for the words "sticky buns" on the Internet to be able to find your Web site in their list of search results—generating you new customers, and of course, new sales. Simple, right?

The problem with this technique is that it has become quite sophisticated over the past five years. In fact, there are now specialized Web firms that strictly handle search engine optimization for businesses, helping them analyze and choose keywords for their business—and helping them to get bumped up as high as possible in the list of search results. The competition for getting listed at the top of a search has become a highly complicated "game" with intricate rules that have developed between Web site owners and search engines.

Getting Help with Search Engine Optimization

If you feel that search engine optimization is critical for the success of your Web site, consider hiring a professional. There are now Web marketing experts out there that can help you navigate the sophisticated search engine optimization game. While it may cost you a few dollars, you'll be glad you did it.

Another avenue is the "search engine optimization" packages currently offered by some Web host services. Check out your host and see if they offer this option, or visit www.networksolutions.com to see a sample package.

As a result, there's no need for you to try to master this complex web of rules (pun intended!). All you need to do is add the basic keywords to your Web site.

Every Web site that is published is allowed to include several free keywords and a one-sentence description of the business on each of the pages—and you should definitely do this, at a minimum. These are called the metadescription, metakeywords, and metatags. You can do this in the "Properties" section of each page of your Web site (you should be able to find the Properties in your Web hosting account).

Spend a few minutes on your metadescription—the one-sentence description of your business—which is short, and describes your business in twenty-five words or less. This is nothing more than a very basic description of your business and key product or service. For example:

> "Peters Writing Services writes and designs marketing materials, procedure manuals, government proposals, and curriculum materials."

Your keywords, on the other hand, should be single words or phrases, and include (at a minimum) the name of your business, and your key products or services. Twenty to fifty keywords should be enough to cover your basic services, and give you access to some search engine exposure. For my business, I chose keywords such as: Peters Writing Services, Paula Peters, technical writing, writers, marketing, brochures, Web sites, procedure manuals, curriculum, training materials—all words that might trigger a search engine to find me for a customer who needs some assistance.

Once your keywords and description are done, you will have covered the bases for search engines and given yourself a chance to get listed. Keep in mind that it may take several days for your Web site to start showing up in the search engines. Later, you can always change your keywords, or hire a Web specialist to make your search engine strategy more sophisticated.

Don't Forget About Niche Search Engines!

Of course, there are also many "niche" search engines that go beyond the "big three." They specialize in a particular industry, and may lead you to much more qualified leads, because they attract a much more specific group of customers.

For example, if you have a lot of manufacturing customers, you may want to run a smaller pay-per-click marketing campaign on a specialty niche search engine that is used exclusively by manufacturers. There are also some search engines that cater to a different group of users. Check out:

> » *www.ask.com*
> » *www.dogpile.com*
> » *www.webcrawler.com*

And if that isn't enough, you can even find a directory of search engines from around the world at *www .searchenginecolussus.com*.

Pay-Per-Click Advertising

What is pay-per-click advertising? You are probably already familiar with it—whether you know it or not. When you do a search for a specific word on Google, for example, you get a whole list of Web sites in your results. Do you ever notice the highlighted search results on the top or right-hand side of the page? Those are businesses utilizing pay-per-click marketing campaigns. Each one of those sponsors is paying for the right to list their ad on that page, along with that specific search term. However, they don't pay until someone actually clicks on their ad, and enters their Web site.

Here's how it works: you register with one (or all) of the major search engines. Most charge a nominal fee (or nothing at all) to get registered. The three most popular search engines for pay-per-click advertising are:

» *www.google.com*
» *www.yahoo.com*
» *www.msn.com*

To get your campaign started, register and create an account with one (or all) of the major search engines. They will walk you through setting up your option preferences, including:

» Writing the short blurb to include in your sponsored ad
» Choosing your keywords for the search engines
» Setting your bid price for each keyword
» Setting your monthly spending limit
» Publishing your campaign "live"

 Keep Track of Your Sales—and Where They Came from

It's a good idea to keep track of the sales you get through your pay-per-click marketing campaign (or any other marketing campaign, for that matter). Whenever a new customer makes a purchase, ask them how they found you: "How did you learn about us?" Then keep track of their answers. You can track them in something as fancy as an Excel spreadsheet, or as simple as a scratch piece of paper with check marks after each of your marketing campaigns— Yellow Pages ad, direct mail postcard, Internet, word-of-mouth, etc. When it's time to evaluate your marketing, you can say with confidence, "Holy cow! I got more leads this month on the Internet than through my Yellow Pages ad. How can I get more?"

The good news about working with pay-per-click marketing is that most search engines only charge you money when someone clicks on your ad. Not only that, but you can limit the amount you spend every month— to as little as $10, if you want. At Peters Writing Services, we often cap our spending at thirty dollars a month, which is plenty to net us about five or six leads for our particular business. This means that if 1,000 people see your ad when they do a search, but no one clicks on it, you don't pay any money. If one person clicks on your ad that month, you will pay for that particular click—in our case, this is somewhere around twelve cents.

You can even set the rates you pay for each click. Generally, the more you pay per click, the higher your Web site appears in the search results (although there is more involved in the search results positioning than that; part of it is also calculated by your relevancy to the topic as well as your keywords). So, if you are trying to get listed at the top of a *very* popular keyword, such as "marketing," then get ready to open your wallet—because you will need to pay a lot per click to be listed at the top of a three-page list of sponsored ads.

Once you set up your account, you will also see other options for advertising you may want to try, such as Google's AdSense program. Remember, there is no hard and fast rule about what works for good, solid advertising. Whatever brings you leads (and doesn't break the rules) is valid!

 ## Look for Promotions!

All three of these large search engines offer periodic discounts on their pay-per-click advertising, sometimes up to as much as $50 or $100 in free clicks for signup. Look for a discount promotion, and take advantage of it. Your Web host may also offer a pay-per-click coupon to one of the "big three" as well.

Once you have established an account and have used it for at least a month, check back on it regularly. See how many people are viewing your ad and how many people are actually clicking through to it. Ask yourself every few months, "How much am I spending on these ad words? Should I increase—or decrease—my spending on the ads?" If you are not getting good leads, try tweaking a few different things and see if you get better results. For example, switch up your:

» Ad blurb
» Keywords
» Bid price

If you are getting *lots* of good leads from your pay-per-click marketing campaign, you may want to expand it. There are a few ways to do that:

» Increase your spending limit on your existing campaign
» Add more/new keywords
» Bid higher on your current clicks (to be positioned higher in the search results)

 Should I Hire a Professional to Manage My Internet Marketing Campaign?

You can, but you don't have to. Many Web design firms are now specializing in setting up (and even tracking) Internet marketing campaigns. Your Web host may even offer a package to do it for you. However, if you have the time, and are willing to do a little bit of experimentation on your own, you can easily manage it yourself. If you don't have the time, interest, or energy, hire a professional—you'll be glad you did.

Again, good marketing is all about experimentation. See what works for you. Try it for three or four months, invest a few dollars in it, and see if you get good leads (and sales) from it. Personally, I try marketing campaigns for a year before I decide whether they are worthwhile; sometimes, one season is better than another. Creativity and experimentation are the key.

Large Online Marketplaces

Many people still think that eBay is an online hobbyists' haven. They are wrong. If you have old and outdated ideas about eBay, and you are selling products on your Web site, it's time to refresh them. Online marketplaces like eBay are not just places for swapping antique Pez dispensers; they are now real places of business selling brand-new products every day through online mini-stores, maintained by entrepreneurs across the globe.

There are many advantages to marketing your products through these online marketplaces. For one thing, you can reach many more buyers than you can with your own online store. Even if you sacrifice a little bit of personalized branding, you are often able to maintain your own storefront, and can customize its appearance. Not only that, but you gain instant credibility with potential new customers. Online marketplaces allow you to reach a whole new audience that you may never have found through search engines—because the buyers weren't looking there. This is a powerful tool for reaching your audience.

Setting up an online store through one of these large marketplaces is simple, and each one offers detailed, step-by-step instructions. What you need to do:

1. Create an account with one (or many) online stores.
2. Customize your storefront, using their templates.
3. Add your products (including descriptions, pictures, and pricing).
4. Begin reaching new customers.

Popular Online Marketplaces for Marketing Your Products

You may decide to market your products through a single online marketplace—or through several. It's your choice. And remember, marketing through an online marketplace does not disqualify you from reaching customers through your own online store, but it can help you reach a whole new group of customers who may never have found you on their own.

Here are a few of the most popular:

» *www.ebay.com*
» *www.amazon.com*
» *www.shopping.com*
» *www.sell.com*

Even if you are determined at this point that you only want to sell your products through your own, personalized online store, consider trying out a larger marketplace for three months, and see what happens. Do you reach a lot of new customers? Is the marketing opportunity worthwhile?

If you go this route, evaluate your sales on these marketplaces at the end of three months, and determine whether it is worth pursuing for another three. Remember, you can always shut down your store if you don't like it. But if you are selling a lot of products and reaching a lot of new customers, it may be worthwhile. If it does not sell a lot of products for you after three months, maybe it's time to focus on another marketing avenue. Or, maybe you'll want to modify your storefront by changing your product display or your templates and try again. The choice is yours.

Blogs

If you are working in an industry that has avid fans—such as gardening, electronic repair, weather, or computers, for example—then you may benefit from marketing your business through a blog. The wealth of information and continual flow of new ideas, discussion topics, and remedies will bring new customers to you through Internet searches—and keep your loyal customers coming back to you, again and again.

Through the use of a blog or online forum, you can share ideas with your customers—and they can share ideas with each other. This can include just about any topic, such as:

- » Fix-it ideas
- » Money-saving tips
- » Hot industry news
- » Do it yourself ideas
- » How-to information

But beware—an inactive blog or forum will make your site look old and outdated. If you don't have the time to regularly update it, or if it is not getting enough activity from your customers to be regularly refreshed, it may do more harm than good. It makes your business look as if it is no longer operating.

However, if you have at least an hour a week (or a month) to devote to updating it, it may be worth your while. For more details on creating a blog, check out the section on "Blogs" in Chapter 4, "Add Other Functions to Your Web Site."

Tell Your Existing Customers About Your New Web Site

If you already have an established customer base, use your Web site to market your business to your existing customers. It's a great way to keep them educated about your product and service offerings, and to remind them that you are available and ready to serve them. Because, let's face it, customers get distracted. It's important to keep them updated on what's going on with your business. And your Web site provides a wonderful opportunity to do that.

How do you do this? By using your Web site as a source of deals, offers, new information, newsletters, blogs, even podcasts—that keep your customers returning back to you. By doing this, they not only learn more about you, your business, and your other services, but they also turn into repeat customers—the most valuable kind of customer you can have.

Let's say that you already have a few customers. Maybe you have two— or maybe you have 200. You are getting ready to sell a new product that you just *know* some of them would love. But—which ones? And, how can you educate them about it, quickly and cheaply?

The answer is: by using your new Web site to inform your existing customers about those new products and services. Here are a few ideas for you to try.

Idea #1: Send an Announcement About Your New Web Site

Here is the basic concept: the more your customers learn about you, the more likely they are to buy from you. And what a great excuse to get your customers to visit you—by announcing your Web site, and inviting them to take a peek. Better yet, ask a few of them for feedback about it; that will guarantee that they actually spend some time looking at it. You may be surprised at what interesting ideas you get back!

Beware of Spamming!

Be very careful about how you send e-mails to multiple recipients. More and more Web hosts are tightening their restrictions on "spamming." The best—and safest—way to send e-mails like this is one at a time, e-mailed directly to your recipient. However, if you have too many customers to realistically send multiple e-mails, and you will be doing mass e-mailings to your customers often, consider purchasing a customer relationship management (CRM) software or service that can handle mass e-mails and still be compliant with spam regulations. A few to check out:

» *www.constantcontact.com*
» *www.act.com*
» *www.salesforce.com*

Announcing a Web site is very easy—and cheap. Simply write a short e-mail and send it to your customers. Make sure to include a link to the Web site directly in your e-mail. For example:

Hi Joe,

I wanted to drop you a note and tell you how excited we are that Peters Writing Services has launched its first Web site! You can see our new online "home" at *www.peterswriting.com*.

I would love to hear your feedback—on our content, services, layout. After you take a look around, please drop me a note.

Thanks!

Paula Peters
Peters Writing Services, Inc.
Phone: (913) 485-4537
www.peterswriting.com

Of course, you are not limited to using an e-mail—you could send an announcement by letter, postcard, or flyer. But by sending the announcement by e-mail, you give your customers the opportunity to click into the site *immediately*, and give you feedback easily by replying to your e-mail. You will have a higher success rate at actually getting your busy customers to visit your new hotspot when you send the announcement by e-mail, where they can quickly see any special features you may have added—such as a blog, special offer, or newsletter.

Idea #2: Point Their Attention to a New Service or Product

As soon as you have a new product or service available, let your customers know. You never know what might interest them. Of course, you don't want to be a pest—but you want to be as helpful as possible, and one of your new Doohickeys may be exactly what they have been needing.

If you are launching a new product or service—or even if you have a current one that very few of your customers know about—why not send out an e-mail announcing it? You can then point your customers to the exact page where the service or product is listed by including that specific URL link in your e-mail, ensuring that they find it right away without clicking around.

For example, here is an e-mail specific to our proposal writing services:

Hi Darien,

I am writing to tell you that Peters Writing Services is now offering government proposal writing services to our customers. In fact, we have written several winning proposals for companies across the country in the past twelve months. You can view samples of our proposals and a description of our new service at *www.peterswriting.com/ governmentproposalwriting.asp*.

If you are interested in learning more, please call me at (913) 485-4537.

Thanks!

Paula Peters
Peters Writing Services, Inc.
Phone: (913) 485-4537
www.peterswriting.com

Notice that I included a direct link to my proposal writing Web page in the body of my e-mail. All you have to do is:

1. Go to the Web page you want your customer to see.
2. Copy the Web address that displays at the top of your Web browser.
3. Paste that address into the body of your e-mail.

Make certain that the link in the e-mail is active and working before you send it, by testing it. Just click it one time to make sure it takes you to the right Web page. As long as that works, you're doing fine! (If it doesn't work, try cutting and pasting the Web address again.) After all, if customers are interested, but can't click through to see it *immediately*, they will likely forget about it . . . and your effort will go to waste. So much of Internet and e-mail marketing is based on curiosity and impulse.

People say to me all the time, "But I've had that service available for months now! It's not really a new service anymore. I can't really justify sending my customers an e-mail about it." And I say—hogwash. Notice that my service had been in full swing for a year before I announced it. Why not? It's simply an education process for your current customers. You are helping them find the services and products they need—before they look for a competitor!

Idea #3: Offer a Special—Only on Your Web Site

A great way to get customers to visit your Web site is to offer a special that is only available online. In fact, two of my favorite hometown businesses—Andy Klein Pontiac (*www.andyklein.com*) and Family Tree Nursery (*www.familytreenursery.com*)—offer rotating special coupons on their Web site *every week*. As people browse for their coupons, they get to see whatever other neat new things they might have available for purchase.

You can do the same thing. Create a special that's available only on your Web site. It may be a coupon, a free shipping deal, or a reduction in service rate for longtime customers—there are hundreds of options to choose from. Whatever it is, announce it via e-mail, postcard, or flyer—the point is to get these customers back to your site again and again.

 ### Great Ideas for Special Offers

A special offer is something of value that you can offer to your customers for a limited time only. Be sure to specify exactly what they are receiving—including any limiting terms—and the deadline when the offer expires (for example, "Good through May 15th" or "Valid until Christmas"). Don't make the mistake of offering an unlimited deal!

Here are a few ideas—use your own creativity to imagine the best one for your business:

- » Free trial membership
- » 25 percent off initial assessment
- » Money-back guarantee for thirty days
- » Free sample
- » 10 percent off your service visit
- » Free gift with purchase
- » Free thirty-minute consultation
- » Free shipping

You can also try changing it up from time to time. If customers know that there will be a regular special offer, they'll come back again and again.

It's a great way to get customers to educate themselves about your business over time.

Idea #4: Rotate Content on Your Home Page

If you think your customers will be visiting your Web site often, it may be worth your while to spend some time rotating the content on your home page. Why? Because every time they visit, they will learn something new about your business, whether that's a product, service, or fancy feature they might enjoy. Even if you only sell four products, and you want your customers to know what's great about them—you could highlight a different benefit or feature every month.

Most businesses avoid doing this because it costs a lot of money to have a Web designer continually rewrite, revise, or move content on their Web site. However, since you are the master of your own Web site, you can do this easily and cheaply. A simple investment of an hour a month to plan, write, and publish a new home page can give you the opportunity to show fresh content to your customers on a regular basis. Remember, you don't have to change your page layout—only the content, which takes significantly less time.

When Does It Make Sense to Rotate Your Home Page Content Regularly?

» When you have a large number of repeat customers regularly visiting your Web site (such as to use blogs, forums, or Webinars)

» When you have the type of business where you get one-of-a-kind products in for sale that you want to show off (and sell) quickly (for example, an import business, antiques business, or a rare book dealer)

» If you have a large number of products or services in stock that you want customers to see, but are "buried" right now in your store

» If you are an artist, architect, writer, or designer that wants to feature new works regularly

Of course, you don't *have* to have one of these reasons to do it. If you enjoy working on your Web site, and like showing off your products and services to your customers—do it! It will be an inexpensive, easy marketing enhancement for your Web site.

Idea #5: Share New Information

Maybe you know a lot about your industry. Or maybe you just have some great ideas for how your customers can save money, stay in compliance with tax regulations, or decorate their home. If you have some insider expertise in your field of business, you can share that with your customers through your Web site. It's an easy way to get people interested in revisiting your site, over and over again.

There are several easy ways to do this. One way is with an e-newsletter (see below). You can also post industry articles (make sure to get copyright permission first), lists of ideas, how-to information, and tips for using your products in the best way possible. You can even write your own articles, and post them directly to your Web site. The best option in this case is to add a separate page, using your standard page layout, called "Helpful Hints" or "Tips" or "Just for You."

The key here is to make the information interesting and appealing to your customers. You will also need to change it frequently to make it worthwhile. A single article dated "2008" sitting on your Web site will look old and outdated. If you choose to include this, be mindful of how frequently you add new information—monthly, at a minimum; weekly is best.

Idea #6: Try an E-newsletter

An e-newsletter is a handy, convenient way to educate your customers about you, your business, and your products and services—while also bringing them to your Web site again and again.

 Using an E-newsletter?

If you are going to be using an e-newsletter, consider that you will get many of the same customers returning to your Web site month after month. This would be a great

> opportunity for you to refresh your home page content, or share a special offer with your loyal customers.
>
> Prepare for the release of your newsletter by taking an hour to plan, write, and publish your new content at least three days before its release. This will give you an opportunity to fix any errors and correct any mistakes—before hundreds of pairs of eyes see it!

While a newsletter might sound intimidating, it is actually quite simple. A newsletter is nothing more than a handful of short articles—usually from three to five—that tell your customers more about your industry, your business, or your services. The articles are typically fifty to 150 words long, and the more they address your customer's interests or needs, the better.

There are two ways you can use an e-newsletter to drive traffic to your Web site: You can post the article on the Web site itself on a separate page titled "Newsletter," and send an e-mail announcement that it's available, preferably with a hyperlink directly to the page included in the body of your e-mail. The better way, however, is to e-mail the body of the newsletter—graphics and all—to your customers, and then allow them to interactively click through the articles to get more information on your Web site. Of course, you can also do both—post the newsletter to its own page on the Web site, and send out the newsletter in the body of the e-mail.

Use software to manage the delivery of the newsletters. Some even have newsletter templates you can use. They vary greatly in price and service offerings. Check out:

- » *www.constantcontact.com*
- » *www.act.com*
- » *www.salesforce.com*

 ## Need Help Writing a Newsletter?

For more specific instructions on how to write a newsletter, check out *The Ultimate Marketing Toolkit* (Adams Media,

2006). This book includes step-by-step instructions for creating the articles for a newsletter.

The Value of Consistent Branding

Now that your Web site is up and running, it's important to consider how it will look compared to your other marketing materials. If your Web site looks—or sounds—markedly different from your other marketing materials, such as brochures and ads, then customers may not be clear that they are from the same company. And this kind of "customer confusion" is bad for your business.

For maximum effectiveness, a Web site should have a consistent brand with the rest of your marketing materials. What does this mean? It means that all of the materials in your marketing campaign—including your Web site, brochures, and any ads you may be running—have a similar design and message.

Maybe you've already got a large marketing effort underway. Or, maybe you're just thinking about it. No matter what stage of the marketing game you are at, make sure that you incorporate your Web site as seamlessly as possible into the rest of your campaign—making your company image and message appear smooth and consistent to your customers. This is called "branding," and with a little planning, it should be fairly easy.

Here are a few tips for creating consistent branding when integrating your new Web site into your other marketing materials.

Tip #1: Communicate Your Web Address—Everywhere!

Now that your Web site is up and running, one of the best ways to drive traffic to it is to communicate your Web address—everywhere (and anywhere) possible. Everywhere your logo and business name appear, your Web address should appear also. For my company, for example, that means ensuring that our logo and the name "Peters Writing Services" is followed by our mailing address, phone number, fax number, and Web site address. For example, on a flyer we produced for a seminar at a middle American conference on government proposals, note the reference on the bottom:

Seminar flyer for government proposal conference

Courtesy of Paula Peters and Peters Writing Services, Inc.; designed by Karla Snider, Karla Snider Design

Note the Web address—along with my other standard contact information—at the bottom of the page. This later helped two attendees to look up my Web site and contact me, resulting in longtime client relationships.

A few places where you'll want to be sure to publish your new Web site address:

» Ads
» Business cards
» Brochures
» Trade show booths
» Flyers
» Mailers
» Billboards
» Radio spots
» Yellow pages
» Company vehicles

Don't forget some of the more obvious places! Many business owners forget to include their Web site address on their:

» E-mail signature
» Letterhead
» Invoices
» Official communications

Tip #2: Use Consistent Design Elements

All your marketing materials—across all media, whether it's the Internet, print flyers, or Yellow Pages ads—should now use consistent design elements.

What does this mean? It means that if you are using green and red colors on your Web site, use those same colors in your ad or brochure. No matter how simple your design, stick to the same basic colors, fonts, photos, and images—time after time.

If you have a logo, use it the same way every time. For example, don't stretch it out, or make it skinnier or wider. If you have a tag line, use it consistently with your logo, in the same font and spot—every time.

By creating a consistent look and feel, you will communicate to your customers that you are a reliable, trustworthy company that is serious about business. And that's good for sales!

Tip #3: Deliver a Seamless Message

Your design is not the only thing that needs to be consistent. Your content does, too. No matter what other marketing materials you are using, make sure that your content is as similar as possible. This builds trust in your organization.

How do you deliver a seamless message? Easy! Simply make sure to describe your products and services using similar verbiage; describe your company in the same way; give the same directions to your retail store; list the same contact information (if possible). The more consistent your message, the more comfortable your customer will feel with you when they see your multiple marketing vehicles, whether it's the Yellow Pages or a brochure or a Web site.

Tip #4: Recycle Your Web Site Content and Design

Looking for a shortcut way to delivering a seamless message about your services, across all your marketing materials? Then get even more bang for your buck by "recycling" your Web site content and design.

If you are considering creating a brochure, flyer, newsletter, ad, or even a press release, you can pull chunks of your Web site content and reuse it. In fact, with a little bit of fiddling around, you can take the exact same design elements—colors, photos, layout—and reorganize them for another media.

For example, the content for your five-page Web site is an almost perfect fit for the layout and format of a trifold, 8.5" x 11" brochure, which has six panels. The content is already written—the design elements are already established—so you can use a graphic design software to lay out your brochure. While you will need to shorten the content to make it fit the new format, you can just change the titles and lay it out, one page per panel—then design a nice cover with your company name and logo.

Another great opportunity to recycle is using a direct-mail postcard. You can include your products and services content on the front side, your contact information on the back side, leave a space for the customer's mailing address, and you're done! Instantly recycled marketing messages.

Chapter 10

WHEN TO HIRE A PROFESSIONAL . . . AND WHY

O kay, okay . . . you read through this book, did all the exercises, created your Web site map, considered the designs, bought your domain name, and you are still stumped. It happens to all of us from time to time. And it's nothing to be ashamed of.

Creating a Web site is not for everybody. No matter how simple the steps, sometimes it's just not right for you. And that's okay. There's no reason you *have* to do it yourself. After all—you're the boss! The final decision is up to you.

If you read through this book, and you know that you absolutely do *not* want to create your own Web site, but you know that you definitely *need* one, then the choice is clear: it's time to hire a professional.

Entrepreneurs do this all the time; we all must "farm out" work that we don't perform very well ourselves. It's one of the keys to successful business ownership. There are some very good reasons for not tackling your own Web site. Read on for a discussion.

Good Reasons for Hiring a Professional

There are several good reasons for hiring a professional, instead of writing, designing, and publishing the Web site yourself. And there is no reason to feel guilty about any of them.

The Top Three Reasons for Hiring a Web Professional

1. You don't have time to do it yourself.
2. You need a fancier Web site than what is described in this book.
3. You just don't feel like it.

Reason #1: You Don't Have Time

If you are so busy between work and home that you do not have even one day to create your own Web site, you should hire out your Web site creation. You may simply be so busy servicing clients, or designing products, or hiring new staff, or getting your store set up, that one day could throw off your whole month. If that's the case, it's time to hire a professional.

There is nothing to feel guilty about if you decide to go this route. Every successful business owner (myself included) must hire out work from time to time. That's part of running a successful business. Do whatever you need to do to get the job done. And don't feel guilty about spending the money—it will be well worth it, just like it is when you pick up that takeout food rather than cooking your own meal.

Reason #2: You Need a Fancier Web Site

Many times, people create their own Web site and realize, "This Web site is a good start, but I need something a little fancier for my customers/ industry." That's completely fine, too. While the basics may work fine for some businesses, depending on your needs, it may not work for you at all.

There are a lot of reasons why you may need a more complex Web site. Perhaps you are opening up your business in an industry where your competitors use Flash animation; or perhaps they all have complex, virtual 360-degree tours of their facilities (such as in the motel industry). Or maybe you are selling a very large number of products online, and could benefit from an interactive virtual catalog. Or, perhaps you would just like something with much more content and intensive graphic design then I've laid out here.

Whatever the reason, it will be worth your while to establish a budget, then talk to a few Web professionals to see if they can execute your vision for the budget that you have. See if they can do what you want for the amount you have to spend. If they can't, they will tell you—and you can always scale back your ideas, increase your budget, or come back to the book and do it yourself later.

Reason #3: You Just Don't Feel Like It

Don't discount this reason. There is a lot of power in your emotions. If you just don't feel like it, don't do it. That's a perfectly good reason to hire a professional.

Perhaps you've read through the book, and you really want to create your own Web site—but you've realized that this is just not going to be any fun at all for you. Don't force it! You'll only hate working on it, and will probably put it off, get frustrated, and then dislike the result in the end, anyway.

There are a lot of tasks that I tried doing myself during my first three years in business—such as my legal contracts, bookkeeping, taxes, office management work. Later on, I realized how much better it was for me just to hire a professional. It saved me time, and a lot of negative energy fighting against it, and procrastinating—energy that I used effectively to go out and find more clients.

How to Hire a Good Web Professional

Deciding that you would rather hire a Web professional is the hard part. Once you have determined that, finding one that can do the work should be rather easy. There are plenty of good marketing and Web design firms out there. No matter how remote your location, you can usually find one through your Yellow pages, chamber of commerce, or even on the Internet.

Hiring a good Web professional is a lot like finding the right employee: you need someone who is good, can do it for the price you can pay, and in the timeframe you need it—and who you enjoy working with. You should expect to interview at least two Web firms, if possible, to get a feel for the different styles and options that come with this decision.

But no matter what you decide to do—whether you tackle the Web challenge by yourself, or you hire a professional to do the work for you— you can use this book as a guide and a reference point to help educate you and walk you through the process. Now you know exactly what the Web designer or marketing firm is going to do for you—and you will be a better buyer because of it.

How can you hire the right professional? And how can this book help you do that?

Here are a few key areas that can tip you off immediately to know whether the firm you are considering is right for the job.

Five Things You Can Do to Hire the Right Professional

Here are five easy things you can do to make sure you get the right one— all with the help of this book:

1. Ask for a Web site map (or better yet, bring one of your own).
2. Communicate reasonable goals for your site.
3. Make sure the approach works for you.
4. Ask for samples.
5. Understand their Web marketing strategy.

Ask for a Web Site Map

After reading Chapter 2, "Plan a Web Site for Your Business," you know that the most efficient way to create a solid Web site is to first do some planning. And a big part of that planning is creating a Web site map.

When you are working with your professional Web designer, ask him to create a Web site map to show you how they plan to approach your Web site. Or better yet, bring your own copy, if you have already drafted one. You will minimize design expenses, and get a more accurate result if you can both agree on a site map in advance.

Communicate Reasonable Goals for Your Web Site

So you need a good Web site, but you don't need one as big as eBay. Right? Then don't allow yourself to get "oversold" on what you need.

Web sites are a lot like cars. You may need one that just takes you to work and back, or you may prefer one that looks really flashy and impresses your friends. It doesn't matter which one is right for you, just be sure that your budget can accommodate your preference. Because if you make your Web site flashy enough, it *will* cost as much as a car.

The bottom line here is that if you don't set reasonable goals for your Web site and for your budget, you can get talked into a lot of bells and whistles that you don't need—at a moment of weakness (e.g., you *desperately* need that Web site up and running before you set up your booth at the trade show on Tuesday). This is not unlike showing up on a car dealer's lot the day after you've crashed your own car. You may be tempted to buy more than you really need, and the car dealer may sense that.

However, if you want thirty pages with flash, animated hyperlinks, and video animation, and you can afford it, and you feel it will impress some of your customers enough to buy your services or products, then go for it.

But if you have a tight budget, tight timeframe, and only need a few pages, say "Thank you, I'll get back to you," and hold out for another bid from a different professional who understands your goals and agrees to stick with them. There are plenty of people out there creating Web sites who can honor your needs and preferences—there is no need to work with someone who doesn't.

Make Sure the Approach Works for You

After reading this book, you know what a Web site should look like, read like, and how it should be published. No matter how fancy it gets, it all comes down to only three main elements:

» Writing
» Design
» Publishing

Ask the Web firm how they will handle these three things. Do they have writers and designers on staff? Or, will they subcontract out these functions? How will they get the content information from you? Did they ask you for your preferences with color, photographs, and content presentation?

There are no right or wrong answers to these questions. It doesn't matter whether the writers work as employees or contractors. What's important is that the Web firm should actively ask you for your preferences to each of these items, and that their approach feels comfortable to you. If something feels "wrong" in how they want to handle these elements, it's probably not a good match.

Ask for Samples

A good Web firm should be able to show you at least three or four samples that are similar to the Web site you have in mind—whether that's five simple, no-fuss pages with light text and minimal photos, or twenty high-end, flash-loaded interactive pages with lots of photos and design elements. If they are a newer firm and explain that, the price of the site should be lowered accordingly.

Don't ever be shy to ask for samples or customer references. Any reputable firm should be able to provide these. I am hesitant to work with a firm that cannot provide samples or references, yet I know several of them who intimidate new customers into working with them just by their big price tag. And *definitely* do not work with any Web firm that does not even have their own Web site up and running. That's a little like hiring a landscaper with no garden of her own.

Understand Their Web Marketing Strategy

If Web marketing is an important part of your strategy, ask your Web professional whether they provide this service—and if so, how it will work. Ask them to describe their approach in your interview with them. (All your candidates should be happy to give you at least one interview with them, either by phone or in person, to describe their process, and possibly show you samples.) How will they do a pay-per-click ad campaign? How will they optimize your Web site to enable the search engines to find you? If you need a good Web marketing strategy, the answers to these questions will be important to you.

 ### Doing an Interview with a Potential Web Design Firm

Just like with a potential new employee, you will want to interview a potential Web design firm that you are considering. Most reputable Web design firms will do at least one interview with you to gather your requirements for your Web site before submitting a proposal to you. A proposal could take anywhere from one day to two weeks to receive, depending on how popular—and busy—the design firm is.

However, don't expect to get endless free consultation time from your Web designer. Like any good professional, their time is their money, and one freebie meeting is probably the most you can expect to get.

If marketing strategy is important to you, read up on your options in Chapter 9, "Market Your Business with Your New Web Site." Educate yourself before you sit down in an interview with a Web design firm, so that you understand your goals and how this site will fit into your comprehensive marketing strategy.

The Four Types of Web Design Professionals

As you've no doubt learned from this book, there are four critical aspects to creating a good, working Web site: the writing, the design, the Web publishing, and the Web marketing. This is exactly how professional Web design is structured. In the professional Web design market, most companies start with one key approach—and build on the other three with good staff. My company is a writing firm, for example, and we treat a Web site as a writing project—so we focus on excellence in content, with a little design, publishing, and marketing thrown in. That's how I like it, and it's a good fit for my customers. Many marketing firms treat Web sites like a design project, and spend more time and budget on design; whereas some Web firms specialize in the truly Web functions, like e-commerce, blogs, and hosting; and some hybrid Web marketing firms excel at marketing your site over the Internet, and are really good at making your presence known to your online customers.

The Four Types of Web Service Companies

There are many companies that offer Web services, each with different specialties. Here are the four main categories you will most commonly find, and their specialties:

1. Writing firms—good, high-quality writing
2. Marketing firms—excellent graphic design
3. Web firms—solid publishing, e-commerce, database design, hosting
4. Web marketing—pervasive Internet marketing

None of these approaches is right or wrong; they are simply different. As a business owner, however, you may decide that one aspect of this spectrum is more important to your own customers than all the others, and that will be an important foundation in your decision.

Remember, no matter what you choose to do, you can use this book as a key reference to help you interview the right Web professional—and make the right decision.

 Where Do I Find a Good Web Professional?

Chances are, no matter where you are located, there is a good Web professional, marketing, or writing firm within your reach. Check out:

» Chamber of commerce
» Yellow Pages
» Networking groups
» Referrals from friends and colleagues

Good luck!

 *Appendix*

SAMPLE WEB SITES

Here are some small businesses who've created their own Web sites. These entrepreneurs come from a wide variety of industries, and have used some very creative solutions for getting their message across—and selling their products and services.

Advanced Genealogical Exploration Services

» Debra and Ken Aubuchon
» Web site created using Dreamweaver and ColdFusion software
» *www.ages-online.com*

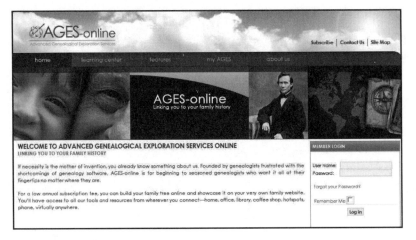

Home page

Courtesy of Deb and Ken Aubuchon, Advanced Genealogical Exploration Services

Features page

Courtesy of Deb and Ken Aubuchon, Advanced Genealogical Exploration Services

Learning center page

Courtesy of Deb and Ken Aubuchon, Advanced Genealogical Exploration Services

Cristy Guy, Fashion + Hair + Makeup Stylist

» Cristy Guy
» Web site created using *www.bizland.com*
» *www.itsallintheclothes.com*

Clients page

Courtesy of Cristy Guy

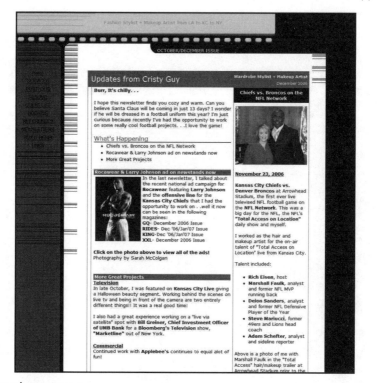

Newsletter page

Courtesy of Cristy Guy

Portfolio page

Courtesy of Cristy Guy

Recycled Eden

» Linda Tamblyn
» Web site created using *www.godaddy.com*
» *www.recyclededen.com*

Home page

Courtesy of Linda Tamblyn, Recycled Eden

Art of recycling page

Courtesy of Linda Tamblyn, Recycled Eden

Custom terrarium page

Courtesy of Linda Tamblyn, Recycled Eden

Teardrop Video

» Joe Padavic
» Web site created using Dreamweaver and Mozilla software
» *www.teardropvideo.com*

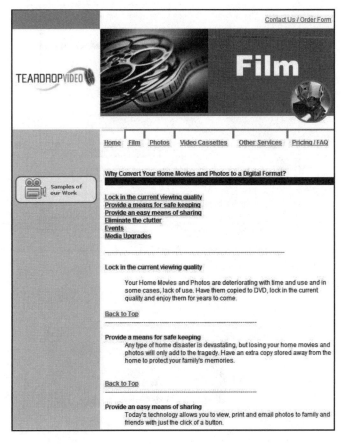

Home page

Courtesy of J. Padavic, Teardrop Video

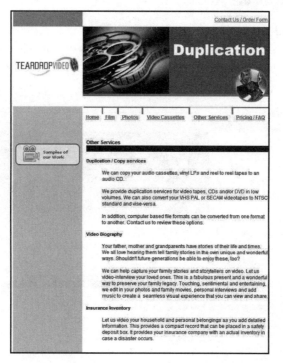

Services page

Courtesy of J. Padavic, Teardrop Video

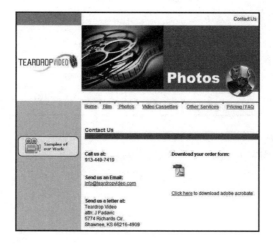

Contact us page

Courtesy of J. Padavic, Teardrop Video

Credentialing Experts, Inc.

- » Diane Lindsay
- » Web site created using *www.godaddy.com*
- » *www.credentialingexperts.com*

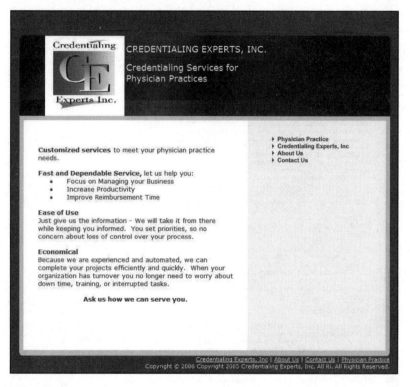

Home page

Courtesy of Diane Lindsay, Credentialing Experts, Inc.

CREDENTIALING EXPERTS, INC.Healthcare Credentialing Services

About Us

• Credentialing Experts, Inc
• About Us
• Contact Us
• Physician Practice

Credentialing Experts, Inc. The increased demands of credentialing regulations, standards, and the need for specialized staff is a burden for many physician practices.

UNIQUELY QUALIFIED STAFF

Double Certified by the National Association of Medical Staff Services (NAMSS), the credentialing professionals organization. Certifications held in both programs, Certified Professional Credentialing Specialist (CPCS) and Certified Professional for Medical Services Management (CPMSM).

Experienced in credentialing for Physician Practices, IPA, PHO, Managed Care, Hospital Medical Staff Office, Ambulatory Surgery Centers and Credentialing Verification Office. Other experience includes Consulting on-site from coast-to-coast and Canada, Credentialing Software Training, Credentialing Audits, NCQA, JCAHO, AOA and CARF Standards, Hiring, Training, and Process Development, work in Medical School and Residency Programs, Physician Recruitment, and Managed Care Contracting. Publication of numerous articles and contributing editor in professional manual.

Professional Association participation on a national, state and local level. Member of the NAMSS Certification Board; Participant on the Job Task Analysis Workshop to assist in the Certification Board and Education Board in a re-evaluation of their programs; local and state office; presentation for the 2003 Annual National NAMSS Conference.

SUPERIOR PROCESSES

Automation for accuracy and efficiency are achieved using one of the leading credentialing software in the country, CACTUS Software. Over half the managed care companies in the country, and many of the largest community and teaching hospitals have used this program for nearly twenty years.

Customized services are designed with your specific needs in mind. Sit down with our professionals and design your own program that meets your temporary or permanent situation.

Call Now For An Appointment.
Credentialing Experts, Inc.
913-851-7780

Credentialing Experts, Inc | About Us | Contact Us | Physician Practice

About us page

Courtesy of Diane Lindsay, Credentialing Experts, Inc.

CREDENTIALING EXPERTS, INC. Healthcare Credentialing Services

Contact Us

▸ Credentialing Experts, Inc
▸ About Us
▸ Contact Us
▸ Physician Practice

Credentialing Experts, Inc.
7301 Mission Road; Suite 141
Shawnee Mission, KS 66208
Phone: 913-851-7780
Fax: 913-851-7785

Name:
Address 1:
Address 2:
City:
State:
Zip / Postal Code:
Country:
Phone Number:
Email Address:
Web Address/URL:
Comments/Questions: Place Comments in here!

Submit   Reset

Credentialing Experts, Inc | About Us | Contact Us | Physician Practice
Copyright © 2006 Copyright 2003 Credentialing Experts, Inc. All Ri. All Rights Reserved.

Contact us page

Courtesy of Diane Lindsay, Credentialing Experts, Inc.

Speech Parade

» Barb Sullivan and Iabil Garza, GaSP Video
» Web site created using *www.yahoo.com*
» *www.speechparade.com*

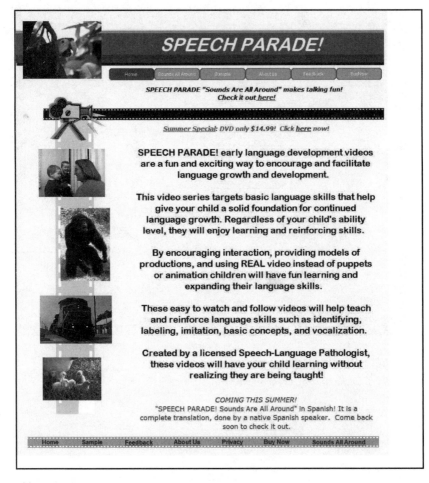

Home page

Courtesy of Barb Sullivan and Iabil Garza, GaSP Video

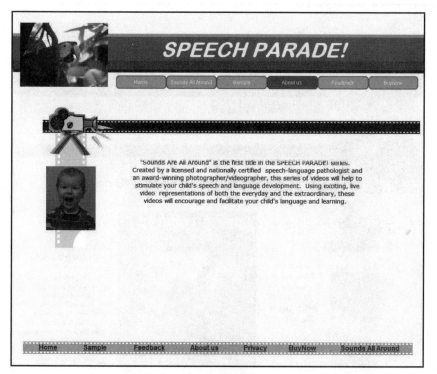

About us page

Courtesy of Barb Sullivan and Iabil Garza, GaSP Video

Buy now page

Courtesy of Barb Sullivan and Iabil Garza, GaSP Video

Education Destinations

» Lisa Weeks and Dale Wheeler
» Web site created using *www.1and1.com*
» *www.educationdestinations.com*

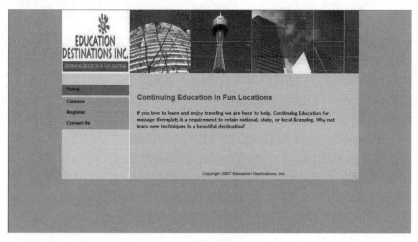

Home page

Courtesy of Lisa Weeks and Dale Wheeler, Education Destinations

Classes page

Courtesy of Lisa Weeks and Dale Wheeler, Education Destinations

Contact us page

Courtesy of Lisa Weeks and Dale Wheeler, Education Destinations

PERMISSIONS AND CREDITS

I would like to thank all the people who shared their time, energy, and intellectual property with me for this book. Each one of these individuals was instrumental in helping to construct this work, through input on content, technical reviews, and use of their Web site knowledge and materials.

Thank you all so very much! I appreciate your permission to use your Web sites, ideas, and materials. It has been such a pleasure working with you.

Debra Aubuchon, Advanced Genealogical Exploration Services

Ken Aubuchon, Advanced Genealogical Exploration Services

Malinda Bryan-Smith, Small Business Development Center, Johnson County Community College

Brody Dorland, Something Creative

Bense Garza, Garza Art and Design

Iabil Garza, GaSP Video

Cristy Guy, Stylist

Lisa Sizemore, Hit Resultz

Mark Havran, Web Guy Extraordinaire

Ryan Humrichouse, Peters Writing Services, Inc.

Diane Lindsay, Credentialing Experts, Inc.

Joe Padavic, Teardrop Video

Mark Short, Transparent Solutions

Karla Snider, Karla Snider Design

Barb Sullivan, GaSP Video

Linda Tamblyn, Recycled Eden

Lisa Weeks, Peters Writing Services, Inc.

Dale Wheeler, Education Destinations

ABOUT THE AUTHOR

Photo by Mark Havran

Paula Peters is a writer, entrepreneur, and the author of *The Ultimate Marketing Toolkit*. Her firm, Peters Writing Services, Inc., specializes in writing procedure manuals, training materials, proposals, and marketing materials for hundreds of businesses across the United States.

Paula is an accomplished speaker and trainer, and delivers hands-on seminars on a variety of topics for business owners, including *Write Your Own Press Release* and *Write an Effective Marketing Brochure*. She has published several articles on business, management, and education for regional and national magazines over the years and has been the recipient of two awards for her work.

Paula is available for speaking engagements and writing projects for businesses and organizations. To learn more, or to contact the author, visit *www.peterswriting.com*.

She lives in Olathe, Kansas, with her husband, Ryan, and son, Zachary.

INDEX